Acclaim for V.S. Naipaul's

A Writer's People

"A bracing, erudite ride. . . . Wonderfully written. . . . One may question Naipaul's premise, but it in no way negates that he is a very great writer. . . . What remains impressive is Naipaul's sense of wonder at the worlds he has discovered." —*The New York Times Book Review*

"This is a brilliant work from a man who more than anybody else embodies what it means to be a writer. . . . As it turns out, Naipaul's reading has been as wide and deep as the peregrinations through the decolonised world that marked the second phase of his career. . . . As ever, Naipaul's sentences are tightly coiled and muscular; they embody the very qualities they praise. . . . Revelatory." —*The Observer*

"Essential reading for those who admire his work and want to understand it further. But there is much there for any enquiring mind, as it offers the insights and observations on literature, history and cultural sensibility of an honest and truly global thinker."

—*The Evening Standard*

"This is an important coda, on a lifetime of 'seeing.' . . . Its most brilliant pages (and the brilliance is still there, even in this late phase) are its most idiosyncratic and individual ones. . . . Its combination and crystallisation of the artistic and the political explains the swiftness with which Naipaul can move from the subject of literature to that of history, from Derek Walcott, Powell and Flaubert to the fascinating chapter on Gandhi and Nehru." —*The Guardian*

"Many sides of the complicated Naipaul personality are on show as he sets them out. There are some amazingly lofty and chilling lines. But there are also explorations of his own woundedness, of his personal myth of origins, or lack of origins. . . . His sympathies come to life. . . . Naipaul is at his best here when teasing out the ironies and complexities of cultural exchange."

—*The Sunday Telegraph*

V. S. Naipaul

A Writer's People

V. S. Naipaul was born in Trinidad in 1932. He went to England on a scholarship in 1950. After four years at University College, Oxford, he began to write, and since then he has followed no other profession. He has published more than twenty-five books of fiction and nonfiction, including *Half a Life*, *A House for Mr. Biswas*, *A Bend in the River*, and *Magic Seeds*, and a collection of letters, *Between Father and Son*. He was awarded the Nobel Prize in Literature in 2001.

Also by V. S. Naipaul

Nonfiction

Literary Occasions

The Writer and the World

Between Father and Son: Family Letters

Beyond Belief: Islamic Excursions Among the Converted Peoples

India: A Million Mutinies Now

A Turn in the South

Finding the Center

Among the Believers

The Return of Eva Perón with *The Killings in Trinidad*

India: A Wounded Civilization

The Overcrowded Barracoon

The Loss of El Dorado

An Area of Darkness

The Middle Passage

Fiction

Magic Seeds

Half a Life

A Way in the World

The Engima of Arrival†

A Bend in the River

Guerillas

In a Free State

A Flag on the Island†

The Mimic Men

Mr. Stone and the Knights Companion†

A House for Mr. Biswas

*Miguel Street**

*The Suffrage of Elvira**†

*The Mystic Masseur**

*Published in an omnibus edition entitled *Three Novels.*

†Published in an omnibus edition entitled *The Night Watchman's Occurrence Book.*

A Writer's People

A Writer's People

WAYS OF LOOKING AND FEELING

An Essay in Five Parts

V. S. NAIPAUL

VINTAGE CANADA

VINTAGE CANADA EDITION, 2009

Published in Canada by Vintage Canada, a division of Random House of Canada Limited, Toronto, in 2009. Published in hardcover in Canada by Alfred A. Knopf Canada, a division of Random House of Canada Limited, Toronto, and simultaneously in the United States by Alfred A. Knopf, a division of Random House, Inc., New York. Distributed by Random House of Canada Limited, Toronto.

Originally published in Great Britain by Picador, an imprint of Pan Macmillan Ltd., London, in 2007.

www.randomhouse.ca

Library and Archives Canada Cataloguing in Publication

Naipaul, V. S. (Vidiadhar Surajprasad), 1932–
A writer's people : ways of looking and feeling / V.S. Naipaul.

ISBN 978-0-307-39694-5

1. Creation (Literary, artistic, etc.). 2. Literature—History and criticism. 3. Naipaul, V. S. (Vidiadhar Surajprasad), 1932–. 4. Authors, Trinidadian—20th century—Intellectual life. 5. Authors, Trinidadian—20th century—Biography. I. Title.

PR9272.9.N32W754 2009 824'.914 C2008-905512-8

Printed and bound in the United States of America

2 4 6 8 9 7 5 3 1

For my daughter,

Maleeha Maria

Contents

A Writer's People

Up to about the age of six or seven I lived mainly in my grandmother's house in a small country town in Trinidad. Then we moved to the capital, Port of Spain, to my grandmother's house in the Woodbrook area. I immediately fell in love with what I could see of the life of the Woodbrook street, and its municipal order, the early-morning washing of the gutters on both sides, the daily gathering-up of rubbish into the blue city-council horse carts. My grandmother's house stood on tallish concrete pillars. It had a front verandah hung with ferns in open metal baskets lined with the netting or bark from the sheathing of new coconut branches at the top of the tree. The ferns made for privacy in the verandah and watering them morning and evening was part of the house ritual. Concrete steps covered by a small pitched corrugated-iron roof led down to the front gate and the pavement. To stand beside the banisters on the steps gave a perfect view of the street and the people. I got to know the people well, though I never spoke to them and they never spoke to me. I got to know their clothes and style and voices.

Sixteen years later, in London, in a darker time, when I had grown to feel that I would never get started as a writer, I remembered the street and the people, and they gave me my first book.

It was a "flat" view of the street: in what I had written I went right up close to it, as close as I had been as a child, shutting out what lay outside. I knew even then that there were other ways of looking; that if, so to speak, I took a step or two or three back and saw more of the setting, it would require another kind of writing. And if, in a greater complication, I wished to explore who I was and who the people in the street were (we were a small immigrant island, culturally and racially varied), that would require yet another kind of writing. It was to that complication that my writing, in fact, took me. I had lived all my writing life in England; that had to be acknowledged, had to be part of my world view. I had been a serious traveller; that had to be acknowledged as well. I couldn't pretend as a writer I knew only one place. There were pressures to do that, but for me such a world view would have been false.

All my life I have had to think about ways of looking and how they alter the configuration of the world.

ONE

The Worm in the Bud

EARLY IN 1949, in Trinidad, near the end of my schooldays, word came to us in the sixth form of Queen's Royal College that there was a serious young poet in one of the smaller islands to the north who had just published a marvellous first book of poems. We had never had news like this before, not about a new book of poetry or about any kind of book; and I still wonder by what means this news could have reached us.

We were a small, mainly agricultural colony and we said all the time, without unhappiness, that we were a dot on the map of the world. It was a liberating thing to be, and we were really very small. There were just over half a million of us. We were racially much divided. On the island, small though we were, the living half-cultures or quarter-cultures of colonial Europe and immigrant Asia knew almost nothing of one another; a transported Africa was the presence all around us, like the sea. Only segments of our varied population were educated, and in the restricted local way, which we in the sixth form understood very well: we could see the professional or career cul-de-sacs to which our education was leading us.

As always in these colonial places, there were little reading and writing groups here and there, now and then: harmless pools of vanity that came and went and didn't add up to anything like an organised or solid literary or cultural life. It seemed unlikely that there were people out there who were guardians of the life of the mind, were watching out for new movements, and could make a serious judgement about a new book of poetry.

But in the strangest way something like that had happened. The young poet became famous among us. He came from the island of St. Lucia. If Trinidad was a dot on the map of the world, it could be said that St. Lucia was a dot on that dot. And he had had his book published in Barbados. For island people the sea was a great divider: it led to different landscapes, different kinds of houses, people always slightly racially different, with strange accents. But the young poet and his book had overcome all of that: it was as though, as in a Victorian homily, virtue and dedication had made its way against the odds.

There might have been other promptings. There was much talk at the time about cherishing our local island "culture"; it was when I grew to hate the word. This talk focused on a talented dance group called the Little Carib (operating in a residential house not far from where I lived), and on the steel band, the improvised and extraordinary music-making of the back streets, done on oil drums and scrap metal, which had developed in Trinidad during the war. With these rare things, it was felt, local people would no longer go empty-handed into the community of nations; they would have something of their own to proclaim and be able at last to stand as men and possess their souls in peace.

Many who looked for this kind of comfort were actually the better-off, middle class and higher, in various ways racially mixed, in good jobs, but with no strong racial affiliation, not wholly African, not European, not Asian, people who had no home but the island. A generation or so before they would have been content to be neither black nor Asian. But now they had begun to suffer in their jobs and in their persons from what, with their success, they saw more clearly as colonial disrespect. They were no longer content to hide, to be grateful for small mercies; they wanted more for themselves.

The talk about a local culture, the steel band and the dance, also came from people with political ambitions. Such talk could flatter a potential black electorate. The franchise was still restricted; but it was known that self-government was coming. Someone who spoke and wrote a lot about the culture was a man called Albert Gomes. He was a city politician who aimed to go higher. He was Portuguese and enormously fat. The fat did him no harm; it made him a character, easily recognisable in the city, much talked about (even in our sixth form), and much loved by the black people in the streets, who at that time, in the 1940s, strange as it might appear, still had no black leader. Albert Gomes saw himself as that leader. As a black leader in the city he had a hard anti-Asian, anti-Indian line; Indians were country people and no part of his constituency. I heard that at one time he smoked a pipe, wore a walrus moustache, and tried to look like Stalin.

Before he came to politics he was a man of culture. In the 1930s and early 1940s he published a monthly magazine called the *Beacon*. He also wrote poetry. At home we had the slenderest book of his poems: *Thirty-three Poems,* four or five inches square, bound in a patterned magenta cloth, dedicated to his mother, "because she does not read verse." I have a half memory of the first poem: *Weep not or wail / Pleasure and grief are vain / The wheel must turn, the river flow / And the day unveil.*

Albert Gomes had a column in the Trinidad *Sunday Guardian*. He signed it Ubiquitous, which not many people knew the meaning of and few knew quite how to pronounce ("you" or "oo," "kit" or "quit"?). He was famous for his big words; it was part of his size and style. It was in a Gomes column that I first came across the word "plethora" and decided it wasn't a word for me. When Gomes wrote about the local island culture he could make it part of his anti-Indian turn, since Indians were staying outside that culture. But there were many sides to Gomes, many strings to his lyre, and I suspect (though I am not really sure now) that it was he who wrote in his vigorous way about the young poet from St. Lucia—part of the theme of an island culture—and made us take notice.

The reader will have guessed by now that the poet was Derek Walcott. As a poet in the islands, for fifteen or sixteen or twenty years, until he made a reputation abroad, he had a hard row to hoe; for some time he even had to work for the Trinidad *Sunday Guardian*. Forty-three years after his first book of poems came out, self-published, he won the Nobel Prize for literature.

As for Albert Gomes, who might have been his champion

in 1949, he came to no good. In 1956, six years after I had left the island, there arose a proper black leader, Williams, a small black man with dark glasses and a hearing aid, stylish (a necessary quality) with these simple props, and soon overwhelmingly popular. He talked a lot about slavery (as though people had forgotten). By that simple means he made all island politics racial; and Gomes, the Portuguese, with no true constituency now, for all his anti-Indian postures, all his talk about the island culture, the dance and the steel band, was broken and humiliated and cast aside by the same black people who just a few years before had liked to see him as a fat-man character, their protector, a local carnival Stalin with moustache and pipe.

SO I KNEW the name Walcott. But I didn't know the verse. Albert Gomes (and others) might have quoted some of the lines in their articles, but I didn't remember anything.

I had no feeling for poetry. Probably language had something to do with it. Our Indian community was just fifty years away from India, or less. I had a Hindi-speaking background. I couldn't speak that language but I understood it; when older people in our joint family spoke to me in Hindi I replied in English. English was a language we were just coming into. English prose was the object of my writing ambition, and such limited feeling as I have now for the poetry came to me later, through the practice of prose.

I didn't do English in the sixth form; and when I saw the text books, the *Lyrical Ballads* and so on, I considered myself lucky. Poetry in school had stopped for me the year before, with Francis Palgrave's *Golden Treasury*. I had loved the rollicking children's verses in the junior reading books at school; more than sixty years later they still come back to me. Palgrave should have built on that pleasure, if I were ready for him; but I didn't get on with his Victorian anthology. I hated the very sight of the red soft-covered book (the soft cover an economy of wartime book-production). The poems he had chosen made me think of poetry as something far away, an affectation, a searching for rare emotion and high language. And just as Albert Gomes had made me decide that "plethora" was never a word I would use, so Palgrave made me decide that poetry was not for me.

So I wouldn't have known in 1949 what to make of Walcott. But we should at least have bought the little book. It wasn't cheap (more than the price of a Penguin, and twice the price of a very good cinema seat) but it wasn't expensive: a local dollar, four shillings and twopence, twenty-one pence in modern money. But if English was something we were just coming to, this kind of book-buying was something we were as yet very far from. We bought school books; we bought cheap editions of the classics; my father, an Indian nationalist in this small way, occasionally went to a shop in Charlotte Street in the centre of the city and bought Indian magazines (the *Indian Review* and the *Modern Review*) and books about India from Balbhadra Rampersad (with his big purple stamp on the fly leaf of the books he sold: I never got closer to him than that stamp: I never got to know the man or his shop). But to go out and buy a new book like the Walcott because people were talking about it would have seemed an extravagance; and that was where we were in the end ruled by the idea of our poverty. And though as a writer I was to depend on people buying my new book, that idea of book-buying as an extravagance stayed with me for many years.

It wasn't until 1955 that I came across the Walcott book. I had been in England for more than four years. They were bleak years. I had done the university (I had read English) and for a year or so I had been living in poor circumstances in London trying to get started as a writer. The only blessing of that time—and it was a very great blessing—had been the part-time job I had by a lucky chance managed to get with the BBC Caribbean Service as editor of their weekly literary programme, *Caribbean Voices.*

Caribbean Voices was a post-war BBC idea, part of a general new dawn in the world, as it seemed, and was about ten years old. I and my father had contributed stories to it, and during my time at the university I had got to know the producer, Henry Swanzy. It happened now that Henry—whose family had or used to have trading interests in West Africa: Henry told me that there was or used to be a famous rum there known as Swanzy Rum—it happened that Henry was going for a few years to Ghana to work in the radio there (part of the new dawn), and it was his charitable idea that I should take over the *Voices* part of his BBC duties.

This rescued me from destitution. I got eight guineas a week minus deductions, and I was required to attend for three half-days a week. In fact, I went in every day, for the excitement, the company of the people at the BBC, and to get away from my two-room lodgings (with shared bathroom) in the Irish area of Kilburn, at the back of the great brick wall of the Gaumont State cinema, said to be the biggest cinema in the country.

I got to know the *Caribbean Voices* archive. I got to know a lot more about Henry's talents as an editor. He was a melancholy man, in some ways too good for the work he was doing; some of his foolish colleagues said he was arrogant. He had had literary ambitions himself at the university, and in the *Caribbean Voices* archive I felt I could see these ambitions sublimated in his work as editor. He took the writing from the islands very seriously. He saw virtue and point where none or perhaps little existed (and it was no accident that, a few years after he left the programme, it faded away, together with the romantic idea of Caribbean writing as a new force in English letters). Henry had a feeling for poetry and language which I didn't have. He might have wanted to be a poet himself; I don't know. His quarterly round-ups of work done on the programme were marvellous; I could never match them. And it was through his quite extraordinary appreciation that I at last came to Walcott and his *25 Poems*, the famous book of 1949, a copy of which I now managed to get.

The copy I got was of the second printing, done in April 1949, three months after the first. I would have left Queen's Royal College by then, and I didn't know at the time that there had been this second printing. It proved now, in a changed time in London, that my memory of the poet's success was not exaggerated. His book (the second printing would have been like the first) was plain and paperbound and thin, almost without a spine, with cream-coloured covers and thirty-nine pages of text. It had been produced without any kind of style or typographical flourish by the Advocate newspaper press of Barbados: a Goudy bold typeface for the titles, a standard news-page font for the poems themselves. A poor job; but the very simplicity was impressive.

My judgement in poetry was good enough for most of what came to *Caribbean Voices*, but it was still crude. I still didn't go to poetry out of choice. But I had a little more confidence now. At the university I had over four years read nearly all Shakespeare and Marlowe, some of the plays many times. This had been an education in itself, training me out of my old idea that poetry dealt in declamation and obvious beauty: some of the plainest lines in Shakespeare and Marlowe had been full of power.

And now, when I went to the Walcott, I was overwhelmed. The poems I could enter most easily were the shorter poems in the collection. They were the ones whose argument I could manage. I lost my way in the longer poems; I thought what was being said prosy and difficult and I stumbled over the poetic diction. I left those poems to one side and concentrated on the ones I liked; the poet and his book, short as it was, did not suffer.

Henry Swanzy had opened my eyes to the beauty and often the mystery of some of Walcott's opening lines. So now I could savour the ambiguity of *Inspire modesty by means of nightly verses,* the first poem in the collection, where the modesty could be sexual or poetic, and the verses could also be prayers; the riddle of *I with legs crossed against the daylight watch;* the delicious word-play of a poem about the recent burning down of Castries, the capital of St. Lucia: *When that hot gospeller had levelled all but the churched sky.* I learned that last poem by heart; though it would be truer to say that I read it so often that it fixed itself in my mind, and parts of it (a little jumbled) have stayed there to this day.

It seemed to me quite wonderful that in 1949 and 1948 and doubtless for some years before there had been, in what I had thought of as the barrenness of the islands, this talent among us, this eye, this sensitivity, this gift of language, ennobling many of the ordinary things we knew. *The fishermen rowing homeward in the dusk are not aware of the stillness through which they move.* We lived in Trinidad on the all but shut-in Gulf of Paria, between the island and Venezuela; that sight of fishermen, silhouettes in the fast-fading dusk, so precisely done, detail added to detail, was something we all knew. Reading these poems in London in 1955, I thought I could understand how important Pushkin was to the Russians, doing for them what hadn't been done before. I put the Walcott as high as that.

I added to my income in those days by doing little five-guinea five-minute radio scripts for a magazine programme on the BBC Caribbean Service. I thought I would do something about the National Portrait Gallery, and I went to see David Piper, the director, who also wrote novels under the name of Peter Towry (one of which I was to review three years later for the *New Statesman*). For some weeks the previous year, 1954, when I was stiff with asthma and a general anxiety, I had done a petty cataloguing job for the Gallery (of *Vanity Fair* caricatures by Spy and Ape and the others, fascinating to me) for a guinea a day, or half a guinea a half-day. David Piper rebuked me now—gently, but it was a rebuke—for showing no interest in the pictures in the Gallery when I worked there. I told him I had not been well; he was magnanimous, and helpful with my little radio script.

I was full of Walcott at this time. I told Piper about him, and recited the poem about the burning down of Castries, "A City's Death by Fire." He, handsome and grave behind his desk, listened carefully and at the end said, "Dylan Thomas." I knew almost nothing about contemporary poetry, and felt rebuffed and provincial. It was a let-down: perhaps, after all, I didn't truly understand poetry. But it didn't lessen my feeling of kinship with Walcott or my pleasure in the lines I liked.

I recited another poem one lunchtime to Terence Tiller, a Third Programme producer I used to see in a BBC pub and had got to know. He drank Guinness in quantity at lunchtime, standing at the bar; he said it was food. He had been a minor poet in the 1940s; I had seen his name in illustrious company in various magazines; and to me in 1955 that was achievement enough. I respected his education and intelligence and generosity. The poem I recited to him was "As John to Patmos," in which, quite wonderfully, as I thought, again ennobling us all, Walcott had equated the light and clarity (and fame) of the Greek islands with what we had always seen about us. It was a poem about the splendour of our landscape, and Henry Swanzy had picked out the extraordinary phrase *the sun's brass coin in my cheek*, which everyone among us who had been to the beach would have recognised.

Terence, like David Piper, listened carefully. The Guinness flush left his face; his eyes were intent behind his thick-rimmed glasses; he was all at once a man to whom a poet's words mattered. His admiration was more wholehearted than David Piper's, and at the end his only comment was on the last two words of the twelfth line: *For beauty has surrounded / These black children and freed them of homeless ditties.* The poet, he said, hadn't yet earned the right to use a word like "ditty."

I was puzzled by this, which seemed a very fine kind of poetic judgement, beyond me, but I respected it, and over the next few weeks I worked out that Terence perhaps meant that "ditty" belonged to a more popular style of writing and could be used to proper poetic effect only in a more sophisticated context. The idea of the physical glory of the islands in the poem was done with standard tropical properties, so to speak, and done without irony; and after all the work the poet had done—the mysterious title, "As John to Patmos," and *the sun's brass coin in my cheek, where canoes brace the sun's strength*—after all that, the "beauty" surrounding the black children had been a strangely lazy word. Picking the poem to pieces in this way, I had to acknowledge that "black," too, had always been difficult for me, embarrassing to recite. This sentimental way of looking and feeling was not mine; "children" would have been enough for me.

But I didn't mind. I could look away from this sentimentality, almost brush it aside. The poet I cherished was the user of language, the maker of startling images, intricate and profound, a man only two years older than I was, but already at eighteen or nineteen a kind of master, casting a retrospective glow on things I had known six or seven or eight years before.

In 1955 I used everything that he sent to the *Voices*, though it was clear that six years after his book the first flush of his inspiration had gone, and he was now marking time, writing to keep his hand in, looking for a way ahead. He did an imitation of a Keats narrative poem; he did something in the manner of Whitman (I believe, but I may be wrong). They were both linguistically accomplished, but they were only exercises, without the island landscape that fed his imagination and was so much part of his poetic personality.

In one poem he tried for a reason I don't remember to recreate Ireland, which I don't think he had visited. I felt I knew why he had done that, and was sympathetic: he would have wanted to be more universal, to break away from the social and racial and intellectual limitations of the island, where, as he had written, *the fine arts flourish on irregular Thursdays.*

It was something we with literary ambitions from these islands all had to face: small places with simple economies bred small people with simple destinies. And these islands were very small, infinitely smaller than Ibsen's Norway. Their literary possibilities, like their economic possibilities, were as narrow as their human possibilities. Ibsen's Norway, provincial as it was, had bankers, editors, scholars, high-reaching people. There was nothing of this human wealth in the islands. They didn't give a fiction-writer or a poet much to write about; they cramped and quickly exhausted a talent which in a larger and more varied space might have spread its wings and done unsuspected things.

It was a kind of literary blight that in varying ways affected other places as well: big countries that for political or other reasons had become hard to write about as they were. So Camus in the 1940s could cleanse Algeria of Arabs; and twenty or thirty years later some South African writers, fatigued by the theme of race, with its inevitabilities, its pressures to do the right thing, could seek to create a race-free no man's land to give room to their private imaginings.

I gave up *Caribbean Voices* in 1956. I lost that intimate connection with Walcott's development, and had no idea how he moved away from the imitative quagmire of 1955. That he would have left that behind I had no doubt.

I met him for the first time in Trinidad in 1960; he was thirty then. He told me one morning in a cafe in central Port of Spain how poems came to him. He did so in a very full and generous way, but what he said was complicated and I couldn't understand. I had looked at a few of the later poems. They did not stir me, though the poet might have said they were profounder than the early poems I knew. The island landscape was there again, but the simple old idea of its "beauty" was dropped; the imagery and the language were more tormented; meaning was elusive. I began to feel—as I used to feel in the old days about all poetry—I was not equipped to deal with this poet.

I met him again in Trinidad in 1965. He was more tormented than before by his job on the local Sunday paper; it would have been humiliating for him to be bossed around by people he saw as his inferiors, in what was still a colonial setting. Yet he had become a kind of local figure. He was doing plays, and they were staged. He took the plots of old Spanish plays (I believe), gave them a local setting, and redid the characters as local Negroes. He was pleased to be asked to do the "book" of a fantasy (for a musical) I had written for a small American film producer. I don't know what he did for that project; the film was never made.

I didn't see him again. He was on the brink of his international career: a wonderful new black voice in the United States: his poems published in New York and London, and called out from the islands to teach in American universities.

THE BOOK OF 1949 is beside me now. The cream soft cover is brown at the edges; though the pages with the poems are in fair condition. The very narrow spine is frayed: more the effect of bookshelf light than of handling. Fifty years on, I see more than I did in 1955.

One of the miraculous phrases Henry Swanzy had singled out for special mention in 1949 was *brown hair in the aristocracy of sea*. I hadn't been able to find that phrase in 1955 in the poems I liked. I found it the other day, more than fifty years later. It occurred in one of the longer poems I hadn't been able to enter. And the phrase wasn't romantic at all, as I had thought, no vision of a young girl seen and loved: it occurred in some coarse lines of rage about white people, foreigners, doing black people away from what was theirs, buying up the beaches of St. Lucia, a local heritage, where the very waves now "kowtowed" to strangers.

Henry Swanzy—a friend of Africa in an old-fashioned way: I heard him speak once of "the enemies of the African race"—would not have wanted to make much of this side of the poetry. *Caribbean Voices* was for the Caribbean; the BBC short-wave transmission was picked up by various island radio stations and re-broadcast by them; the decencies had to be observed. And it was left to me now, fifty years later, to read more deeply. The brown hair that had stirred the poet was not always in the aristocracy of the alienated sea, beside the private beach. In one poem it was also the hair of a local girl, white or blonde or fair, who had mocked a letter of the poet's. A young man's unrequited interest, important enough (at that time of limited experience) to be worked into a poem: there was a wound there.

I began to understand, all these years later, that the "black" theme of these early poems—those children freed of homeless ditties by the beauty of their island—that Terence Tiller had worried about, and which I had brushed aside in 1955, would have been more important in 1949 both to the poet and the propagators of island "culture" than I knew; and that for those people—poor old fat Albert Gomes with his Stalin moustache, and all the others—the Walcott I had a feeling for perhaps hardly existed: the young man like myself, carrying in his head the landscape I knew, able to fit words to quicksilver emotions, better as a proven writer than I was (who even in prose had hardly written, and was full only of the large ambition in which everything was still possible, a kind of never-never land of literary judgement).

And that idea of the beauty of the islands (beach and sun and coconut trees) was not as easy as the poet thought. It wasn't always there, a constant. It was an idea that had developed during the twentieth century. The British soldiers and German mercenaries who invaded Trinidad in 1797 (and luckily for them took it from the Spaniards without firing a shot) were landed in heavy winter overcoats on an awful black swamp west of Port of Spain, shallow for a long way out, and left to wade ashore. No idea there of local beauty. People who travelled to the islands before the Great War of 1914 didn't go for the sun; they travelled to be in the waters where the great imperial naval battles of the eighteenth century had been fought; or they took in the islands on their way to see the engineering works of the Panama Canal before the water was let in. The sun in those days was something you had to protect yourself against. Photographs of English travellers in Trinidad from that time show the women with parasols and in full many-layered Edwardian dress.

The idea of beach and sun and sunbathing came in the 1920s, with the cruise ships. (Consciously old-fashioned people, like the writer Evelyn Waugh, born in 1903, refused to sunbathe.) So the idea of island beauty, which now seems so natural and correct, was in fact imposed from outside, by things like postage stamps and travel posters, cruise ships and a hundred travel books. It was an overturning of old sensibility, old associations. Until then the islands were thought of as ancient plantations, places of the lash; and that was how, even until the 1950s and 1960s, island politicians, stirring up old pain and racial rage, sought to characterise them.

The sea I always loved, and could be frightened by. It was always staggering, especially if you had to make a little journey to get there: that first sight of it, with the unexpected noise, at the end of a cliff or behind the crisscrossing grey trunks of a coconut plantation. Away from that the land was neutral, just there. I will tell this story. In 1940 my grandmother bought a wooded estate in the hills to the north-west of Port of Spain. The estate house was set in landscaped grounds. My grandmother asked her extended family to come and settle. The first thing they did, for no good reason, and perhaps only out of idleness, was to cut down all the trees on the drive and in the grounds; then they slashed and burned a hillside and planted maize and peas. The land began soon to be eroded. In only a few years it became a black rural slum, little pieces rented out to poor black immigrants from the other islands; and no one grieved.

I don't think in Trinidad we felt as children that we walked in a liberating beauty, like Walcott's black children; perhaps we felt the opposite. Though it might be said that Walcott came from a much smaller island, with the splendid sea always there; and when he thought of landscape it was natural for him to think of the sea and the lovely bays.

It is an unpeopled landscape, though, in that first book. There are no villages, no huts, no local faces brought up close. The poet stands alone. He has a memory of his father, who is dead; a memory of a foreign painter instructor and friend, who is no longer on the island; and, of course, a memory of the rebuff of the fair girl. No one close: there are the far-off fishermen in the sea at dusk; there are the black children, undifferentiated, almost an abstraction, freed of homeless ditties; there are the faceless brown-haired foreigners in the sea, the occasion of jealousy and pain. The poet, churned up by his sensibility, walks alone. Even when for a whole day he walks among the ruins of his city of Castries, burnt down in a great fire, he walks alone, *shocked at each wall that stood like a liar.* He is a kind of Robinson Crusoe, but with the pain of a modern Friday. *I, in my skin prison, in my very joys suffer.* He doesn't really tell us why: the fair girl is not really cause enough. *The day you suddenly realised you were black.* Too innocent really, not to say disingenuous, in 1947 or 1948, a time of segregation and the beginning of apartheid; and perhaps, but only perhaps, that moment of realisation was when he embraced the idea of the black children. It is actually possible to feel that without the black idea, the pool of distress, always available, in which the poet could refresh himself, the unpeopled landscape would be insupportable.

Religion in the early poems is as much a feature as race, and has a similar kind of simplicity. The island is like the Patmos of St. John; and that is a surprising and beautiful conceit. But it is something else when after the great Castries fire Christ walks in the smoking Caribbean sea: this is like the flambeau-lit street-corner preacher of the islands with his white-clad women followers, promising damnation below the shop eaves. The great fire shakes the poet's faith, but only for a few lines; faith returns when he sees the new leaves on the hill, *a flock of new faiths;* it is as simple as that. The harder questions of belief are left alone; and the reader can feel that without religion, without that pool of enthusiasm, that idea of a whole world of love, balancing the pain of the black idea, the plantation New World island, with an unmentionable past, would be utterly bare, a spiritual emptiness that would be hard to write about.

The poet must surely have felt the spiritual emptiness about him. That is probably why, in the early poems, the landscape is unpeopled. It would have been a great problem for the poet, knowing how to go on; and it explains why in 1955, six years after his first book, he seemed (from the material he sent to *Caribbean Voices*) to have come to a kind of halt. The spiritual emptiness was a problem for everyone from the plantation territories who wanted to write. Many were destroyed or silenced by it.

Walcott found his own way around that emptiness. He began to fit his island material to older, foreign work. He might take an old Spanish play, say, and re-work it as a local play: Shakespeare's method. You could say that this kind of borrowing—at its simplest, turning St. Lucia for a few lines into the island of Patmos—gave a solidity to the setting which it didn't have before. It would also have, profoundly, falsified. There is a specificity to writing. Certain settings, certain cultures, have to be written about in a certain way. These ways are not interchangeable; you cannot write about Nigerian tribal life as you would write about the English Midlands. Shakespeare when he borrowed was exchanging like against like. It is the better and truer part of the labour of a writer from a new place to work out what his material is, to wring substance from the unwritten-about and unregarded local scene.

Walcott was lucky in his early audience. They were middle-class people mainly of mixed race who had begun to have some idea of the spiritual emptiness in which they lived. They would not have been able to define that emptiness. Yet it was there, all around them. The beaches of which they were proud, almost as of a personal possession, might have given them an idea of the beginning of the emptiness. If they could have looked at those beaches in another way they might have seen the past in a simple picture: New World islands scraped clean of the aborigines Columbus and his successors saw. This was history, though, far off, not to be looked at too closely, not to be felt in the bones. The unhappy middle-class people would have thought mainly of the later colonial set-up and their place within it, the secure but petty civil-service jobs, the small pay, the general absence of grandeur, the need always to look outside for anything—a film, a book, the life of a great man—that might lift a man out of himself.

The competing empires of Europe had beaten fiercely on these islands, repeopled after the aborigines had gone, turned into sugar islands, places of the lash, where fortunes could be made, sugar the new gold. And at the end, after slavery and sugar, Europe had left behind nothing that could be called a civilisation, no great architecture, no idea of local beauty, no memory of style and splendour (the splendour created by the sugar wealth would have occurred elsewhere, in Europe), only the smallest small change of civility. Everything that remained was touched with the pain of slavery: the brutalities of the popular language, and the prejudices of race: nothing a man would wish to call his own. And when in the 1940s middle-class people with no home but the islands began to understand the emptiness they were inheriting (before black people claimed it all) they longed for a local culture, something of their very own, to give them a place in the world.

Walcott in 1949 more than met their need. He sang the praises of the emptiness; he gave it a kind of intellectual substance. He gave their unhappiness a racial twist which made it more manageable.

Then he went stale on them. He exhausted the first flush of his talent; nothing more seemed to be coming; and he became ordinary, a man in need of a job.

In time he began to work on the Trinidad *Sunday Guardian,* doing a weekly cultural article. He was too good for the job; and in 1960, when I was in Trinidad on a visit, he told me that someone had said to him, "Walcott, you've been promising for too damn long, you know." He told it as a joke, but it wouldn't have been a joke for him. From this situation he was rescued by the American universities; and his reputation there, paradoxically, then and later, was not that of a man whose talent had been all but strangled by his colonial setting. He became the man who had stayed behind and found beauty in the emptiness from which other writers had fled: a kind of model, in the eyes of people far away.

. . .

OTHER WRITERS FROM THE REGION were not so lucky. I will mention three: Edgar Mittelholzer, Samuel Selvon, and my own father.

Edgar Mittelholzer, born more than twenty years before Walcott, in 1909 in Guyana, had a hard, wandering early life. His well-received novel, *A Morning at the Office*, now vanished, was published in London by the Hogarth Press in 1950, the year after Walcott's *25 Poems* was privately published in Barbados. Like Walcott, Mittelholzer was a mulatto, of old mixed race; but, unlike Walcott, he didn't put himself on the black side. Mittelholzer made a great play with his name, sometimes spelling it with the umlaut on the "o." Sometimes he spoke in a general way of a Dutch ancestor, sometimes (towards the end, like a man who had done research on the subject) he spoke of a Swiss ancestor who migrated to Guyana in the eighteenth century. Some of this would, of course, have been true.

The office of Edgar's novel was in Trinidad, the characters a gallery of racial stereotypes, quite shocking to local people; but that was Edgar's Dutch or Swiss way in these matters. Two novels later, Edgar moved to the publishing house of Secker and Warburg. It pleased him then to find that he was not too much darker than his publisher Fred Warburg; it was an unexpected way of judging a publisher. He had begun to write slave-plantation melodramas (race and sex and the whip) set in Guyana, and he wrote as a planter and a Dutchman. His books, *Children of Kaywana, Kaywana Blood, The Harrowing of Hubertus*, had a kind of vogue. But it was or became a crowded field, and Edgar's books have now disappeared.

Every writer of the region has to find a way of going on, of not drying up, of overcoming the limitations of the place. Walcott borrowed Spanish plays and did them over with local characters. The plantation novel was Edgar's way. It gave him room; he liked the idea of the large narrative. He couldn't stay with the quiet Trinidad material of *A Morning at the Office.* That novel, with its simplicities, had said all that he wanted to say, from his special point of view, about the colony. And Edgar might have said that the simplicities, his way of dealing only with the externals of things, matched the setting and the material. There was no depth to go into.

Some time in early 1965—I had long moved away from *Caribbean Voices* and the BBC Caribbean Service and from radio generally—Edgar sent me a little green-covered booklet that had been printed in Trinidad in the late 1940s. The booklet, closely printed and only a few pages long, contained work that had been read to a local writing group. This writing group was the idea of an Irish judge who had arrived in the colony not long before. He provided the drink and the encouragement and would have paid for the printing of the little booklet. There was a story by Edgar in this booklet; a piece by George Lamming, I believe; and a story by my father.

I knew the story well. My father had written it in painful circumstances. We had been reduced at the time to living in one room in my grandmother's house in Port of Spain. It was quite a short story, but I remember how my father had laboured on the writing. The material was precious to him, part of his small store as a writer: an account (which he would have had from his mother) of the wretchedness that attended his birth: his mother chased away by his father and going in her destitution, perhaps walking all the way, to have her child at her mother's. Everyone in this story of 1906 was very poor indeed, unprotected, close to helplessness, no one truly a villain. My father handled this background of poverty and heartache in his own way. He overlaid it with the beauty of the old ritual that had to follow the birth of a child. This would have made it easier for him to write; yet at the same time he must often have thought (though he said nothing) that more than forty years after the time of his story he was still unaccommodated in the world.

The booklet was precious to me. I kept it longer than I should. I suppose I had some idea of having it copied, not as easy then as it became later, and didn't know how to go about it. And then there came a furious letter from Edgar. He wanted the booklet back. He was quite enraged. He couldn't be denied. I sent the booklet back with an apology.

Not long after there came a shocking piece of news. Edgar, who lived in a southern suburb of London, had one day soaked himself with petrol and set himself alight, like a Buddhist monk in Vietnam. I never got to know what had driven him to this, or how he had got the courage and resource. There was a story that he had become a Buddhist, which I would have thought the most difficult thing for an outsider to be; but I don't know how true that was and what it meant, or how it could have converted into the final horror. In this horror there was yet so much awful method: going through his papers, putting them in order (or perhaps wishing only to destroy them), going to the trouble of sending me the green booklet, and then remembering waspishly to ask for it back.

A writer lives principally for his writing. Edgar, whatever might be said about his work, was a dedicated writer. And I wonder whether an idea at the back of his mind during those last days of pain and resolve wasn't that he had got as far as he could with his writing.

Samuel Selvon was a Trinidad Indian. He was born in 1923. He didn't come (like my own family, say) from the more rooted rural Indian community, where an India of sorts could be said to survive. Selvon's Indians were semi-urban people shaken loose from the rural community, and losing their traditions fast. After various wartime jobs Selvon joined the *Trinidad Guardian* and for a time did columns for the evening paper under the name of Michael Wentworth, very suave, very smooth, more like a disguise than a pen-name. In 1950 (four or five months before me) he went to England. In 1951 he published his first novel, *A Brighter Sun*, a simple reconstruction of wartime Trinidad life for a semi-urban Indian. It is hard to be the first with any kind of writing, and Selvon in this book burnt up his simple material.

Trinidad was the subject best suited to Selvon's talent. In far-off London it faded, or he lost touch with it. He had trouble with his second book, *An Island Is a World*. When at last it came it was wordy and absurd, full of poor man's philosophizing about the beauty of the simple life in a simple setting (Selvon denying in this way the purpose of his own migration to England in 1950). He continued in much the same vein in the *Caribbean Voices* studio, where we had asked him to record an interview. The prosiness and piety and self-regard were intolerable. I was young, not yet twenty-three. I heard myself saying, like a pompous Oxford don, "Most laudable." That was the don, and it would have passed. Then, however, I went on with something of my very own: "But getting back to your wretched book—" The words had slipped out. Apology was useless (in spite of Sam's forgiving sweet smile). We were recording on disc, and editing was not easy. The interview had to be scrapped. Forty years later I saw the offending book in an outside stand of the Gloucester Road Bookshop. It was being offered for five pence. I bought it, in a modest act of expiation, and put it on my shelves.

Selvon would have fallen silent if he hadn't alighted on the subject of the black West Indian immigrant in London. He was good with the popular black language; he could make it sing; and in his attractive natural way he did picaresque tales (*The Lonely Londoners,* 1956) which seemed drawn from life but were in fact formal, with their own rules, like Damon Runyon's New York stories or like W. W. Jacob's night-watchman stories from London's old dockland. There was real comedy; the inventive things Selvon did with the Caribbean English language (he did not merely record it) should at least have earned him a place in the anthologies. But this new material, like the old Trinidad material, was limited. There were the same black characters, it seemed, and variations on the same joke (black people knocking hopelessly on white doors in London); and then characters and jokes were overtaken by social change in the black community and in England itself. Eventually Selvon left London and went to Canada. I imagine there would have been some kind of job or subvention there; but for him as a writer this third home would have been a desolation. He died in 1994. He left behind no solid body of work.

My father, Seepersad Naipaul, the third of the writers I wish to mention here, did only a handful of stories. He was born in 1906 and died in 1953. Like Walcott and Selvon many years later, he worked for the *Trinidad Guardian*. Unlike them, he never got away. He started as a country correspondent in 1928 or 1929, specializing in Indian matters, became a general writer, and then with two short breaks stayed with the paper until he died. He began to write stories in 1939, but it was only in the last three years of his life that he found an audience, and modest financial reward, in Henry Swanzy and *Caribbean Voices*. Until then his serious writing was done for himself and out of personal need.

He wrote about Trinidad Indian life. He saw it as self-contained; that was how it would have appeared to someone born in 1906. Unlike Selvon he didn't see the races flowing together, with the Indian side, the language and the ceremonies, gradually being washed away. In my father's early stories the other races do not appear; the Presbyterian head teacher is Indian; so is the missionary. Old ritual is important. It heals pain; it brings together broken families again. This exercise of benign ritual is one of the functions of the village community. My father sees it all as whole, though in a generation or two it will go.

He is possibly the first writer of the Indian diaspora, the first to write of its transplanted people, unprotected peasants, seeking as if by a necessary instinct to recreate the society they left behind, and to a large extent succeeding. It is actually a big, Willa Cather–like subject—my father boldly pushes the story back to 1906, the year of his birth—but it is an Indian subject, and India will never wish to know its history, literary or otherwise, and no one else will. He is nonetheless more of a pioneer than the other writers I have mentioned, and he is more original. To do what he did called for fine knowledge of the old ways, and a gift of modern expression. No one else could have done what he did; and it was all done, a great labour, as I can testify, without recognition.

My father damaged his material when he tried to fit it to what he thought of as "story": the trick ending, say. It was his pathetic wish to get his far-away stories into the magazines in England or the United States, and he thought the trick ending would help. So it happened that in the actual writing he could aim high and then aim low. Because he could think of so few trick endings, and because "story" eluded him, he felt he had little material, and he worked and re-worked the few things he did finish. In fact, if he could have taken a step back, he would have seen that there were more things to write about. If he could have taken a step back from his stories about the beauty of old ritual, and considered the colonial setting, other ideas might have come to him. But probably that step back into the bad colonial setting would have caused him pain, and pain was something he didn't wish to face in his writing.

I often asked him to write about his childhood. I wanted to know. He was a fatherless poor boy farmed out among relations; and from time to time he gave me comic glimpses of that childhood. But he never wrote about it, and he never gave me anything like a clear account. So I never got to know. If we had lived in a place where there was a tradition of writing, the confessional autobiography might have been one of the forms, and my father might not have been so shy of doing his own. But there was no audience for that kind of writing or any other; in a place like Trinidad, with all its past cruelties, to write of personal pain would have been to invite mockery. There is a dreadful story to be told about this kind of mockery. In 1945, when newsreels of concentration-camp sufferers were shown in Port of Spain cinemas, black people in the cheaper seats laughed and shouted. Perhaps behaviour like this—and not always fear or sorrow—attended the bad punishments of slave times.

There was a tradition of complaint in Negro poetry, like the tradition of the blues. It seemed right that this should be so. I was also aware for a long time at school, from books we came upon, about Martiniquan poetry and the like, that this poetry was written about in a special way: not judged as verse so much as expounded, with long quotations establishing the poet's grief or anger. This was the tradition into which the young Walcott was received.

There was no tradition of Indian writing or colonial writing or confessional writing into which my father might have been received. And all the pain of his early life, the material that in another society might have been his making as a writer, remained locked away.

TWO

An English Way of Looking

THIS WILL NOT be an easy chapter for me to do. I got to know Anthony Powell in 1957. He was fifty-two, at the peak of his reputation, and I was twenty-five and awkward, poor in London, with one book published. For a reason I couldn't understand—there was every kind of difference between us—he offered his friendship. It took me some time to believe in this friendship, but it was real, and it continued until 1994, when he was old and bent and walked slowly. He said goodbye then, at the front door of his house in Somerset, and he said so with a certain ceremony that let me know that this was to be our last meeting. So indeed it was, though he continued to see other people.

Six years later he died. I was asked by a television news programme to be interviewed about him. I agreed willingly but then, in the studio, found to my dismay that I had very little to say about his writing. I had to bluff; it couldn't have been a very good item on the evening news. I had been the great man's friend for all those years but had read little of his work.

I cherished his friendship and generosity, delighted in his conversation, thought him well read and always intelligent, but kept on putting off a serious connected reading of his work. Until 1974 he had been writing a many-volumed autobiographical novel, *A Dance to the Music of Time;* after that, when he was past seventy, he had done bits and pieces of fiction and drama. In what seemed like the remote past I had read the first couple of volumes of the big novel. Very little had remained with me. I thought that might have been because the matter, an English upbringing, was too far away from me. Powell was proud of being an English writer; he thought it something delicate and special, something to which people would at some time want to return; and from those two novels an impression (which I didn't trust because of its strangeness) had stayed with me that the writer had wished to show how much he knew of English manners.

A long time afterwards I read the third volume of the series. I was deeply impressed, by the care of the writing, the management of various moods, and the pace. I wrote him a letter of admiration, and I promised myself that one day, when I had the time, I would do that connected reading of the work which I hadn't yet done.

When he died I was asked by the editor of a literary weekly to write about him. I was working on a book at the time and couldn't do anything just then. But the idea of writing about Powell attracted me, and I asked the editor to wait a little. When I was free I settled down to read. I got two of the paperback omnibus volumes, and read six connected books from the middle. I was appalled. Powell had had a little American success with one book, and I felt that this perhaps had corrupted him. There was none of the shape I had expected to find in the longer book. There was less and less care in the writing; everything was over-explained; the matter became more nakedly autobiographical; and there was a strange new vanity in the writer, as of a man who felt he had made it, and could now do no wrong, could now like a practised magician pull his old comic characters out of his hat and feel he had to do no more.

There was no narrative skill, perhaps even no thought for narrative. A moment comes during one of the middle books when a number of the earlier characters are consumed in one evening in a bombing holocaust. In the main narrative, which is full of coincidences that eternally bring many of the old characters together again in every book, this holocaust is like yet another private event, a private blitz, another partial assembling of the cast: two hit-and-run bombers almost without warning destroy two of the houses or places the writer-narrator knows well: two bombers, two houses, no more.

Such a strange event has to be handled carefully by a writer; hints of the calamity and the oddity have to be dropped beforehand, perhaps even for a book or two in advance. It is no use saying that during the war people died like this, and without warning. A book is a book; it has to have its own logic. And the book anyway is being written long after the event, when the awfulness should have been reflected upon and digested. What happens in the book is that some of the people who are going to die behave strangely: they appear to be yielding to some psychic prompting and are saying a long goodbye. And when later in the evening, by accident, the writer learns of the calamity, he, normally retiring, content to be a listener and observer, behaves with unusual energy, finding ways in the blackout of getting to the two bombed houses, one after the other, and confirming what he already knows.

This is how death and knowledge of death comes. The moment should be profoundly tragic. But some emotional charge is missing. What is missing is that we don't truly know the people who have died; we don't know them as well as the writer knows them or their originals; we know only their names. That is one of the consequences of the unwieldy way the book is organised. It is done in the first person from beginning to end, and much of what we learn about people comes through dialogue. It is a ponderous form of narrative and, since every dialogue starts from scratch (and though Powell is a master of the different ways of English speech), it wastes time, giving equal weight to the trivial and the important.

Every volume begins with a piece of what we might call actuality; and every occasion of actuality ends in the most predictable way as a kind of party, where we are given little glimpses of the central people of the narrative and learn how they have fared since we have last seen them. We learn especially about their current mating. In the beginning this provided surprise; but then there is no surprise in this game of musical chairs. And then, too, we begin to feel that these people, though they were new to us in the beginning, part of a social knowledge which we might not have had, are only one-dimensional, not interesting enough for us to follow. Their interplay doesn't become profounder with age and the passage of time. The writer gives them a lot of attention, but we feel somehow that he sees more in them than he makes us see.

This failure is extraordinary. Powell worked for some time as a film script-writer before the war, and in early conversation with me he often used his script-writing experiences to demonstrate how writing should not be done. He and his script-writing colleague (he said) might need to introduce a character at a certain stage. To give this character an identity they might concentrate on externals; that was the easiest way. They might give the man a limp or a blinking eye; or the man might wear a certain kind of clothes, or smoke a certain kind of cigarette or cigar. This method worked in film scripts; it was shoddy in books. And yet it can be said that this in some way was Powell's method in his big book.

My feeling at the end was that this man, my friend, might have written books, might have lived the literary life, but wasn't the kind of writer he wished to be.

And the feeling was strengthened when I looked at one of the pre-war books, *From a View to a Death*. An artist goes to a country house to paint a portrait. English country manners are carefully described: this might almost be the point of the book. The artist then decides to take the country gentry on at what he sees as their own game. He gets on a horse and falls and is killed. And, as in the later books, everything is over-explained; there are too many words. But what is the point? Is it that artists should stick to what they know best? It is mysterious, and perhaps there is no point apart from the display of social knowledge.

There is a kind of writing that undermines its subject. Most good writing, I believe, is like that. *A View to a Death*, for all its care in the delineation of county manners, leaves English social life just where the writer found it. And the same is true of *The Music of Time*.

A COMMON DEVICE OF FICTION is like this. A great man dies, covered in honour. Someone then, usually an admirer, goes into the life to do a biography and discovers all sorts of horrors. Ibsen uses this device a lot, but without the death; every Ibsen great man has near-murder in the background. I felt like a fictional character, but I didn't know how to do the story. I didn't know how to present myself to people who knew Powell. I didn't think anyone would believe that after all the years of friendship I had not read Powell in any serious and connected way, had only just done so, and didn't now think of him as a writer. It was a piece of Ibsen-like horror. It wasn't something I could put to the editor who had asked me to write about him. So I did nothing. I said nothing. But somehow the idea got around that I had dishonoured a friendship.

And it would not have been easy to put to people that the friendship remained of value, was not diminished by the horror. I had met him in 1957 as a great English writer, was flattered by his attention, and through all our friendship I never ceased to think of him as a great writer. It may be that the friendship lasted all this time because I had not examined his work.

MY PURPOSE IN THIS BOOK is not literary criticism or biography. People who want to know about Powell or Walcott can turn to the critical works that have been done about these writers. I wish only, and in a personal way, to set out the writing to which I was exposed during my career. I say writing, but I mean more specifically vision, a way of seeing and feeling.

Romantic and beautiful though the idea is, there is no such thing as a republic of letters where—as in an antechamber to a fairly judged afterlife of reputation or neglect, and in the presence of a literary St. Peter—all bring their work and all are equal. That idea of equality is of course false. Every kind of writing is the product of a specific historical and cultural vision. The point is uncontentious. National histories of literature make it all the time, and no one minds. But the self-serving "writing schools" of the United States and England think otherwise. They decree that a certain artificial way of writing narrative prose (which is a general way now and in twenty or thirty years will almost certainly appear old-fashioned) is the correct way.

Let me see whether I can give a short guide. You begin (at the risk of using too many words, like Hemingway) with language of extreme simplicity (like Hemingway), enough to draw attention to your style. From time to time, to remind people, you can do a very simple, verbose paragraph. In between you can relax. When the going gets rough, when difficult or subtle things have to be handled, the clichés will come tumbling out anyway; the inadequate language will betray itself; but not many will notice after your very simple beginning and your later simple paragraphs. Don't forget the flashback; and, to give density to a banal narrative, the flashback within the flashback. Remember the golden rule of writing-school narrative: a paragraph of description, followed by two or three lines of dialogue. This is thought to make for realism, though the dialogue can't always be spoken. Chinese and Indian and African experience sifted down into this writing-school mill comes out looking and feeling American and modern. These writing-school writers are all given the same modern personality, and that is part of their triumph.

I grew up on an island like Walcott's. Other races were close, but for my first five or six years, in the 1930s, I lived in a transplanted peasant India. This India was being washed away by the stringencies of our colonial life, but it still felt whole, and this gave me a base of feeling and cultural knowledge which even members of my family who came later didn't have. This base of feeling has lasted all my life. I think it is true to say that, in the beginning, living in this unusual India, I saw people of other groups but at the same time didn't see them. This made me receptive to my father's stories of a self-contained local Indian life and the healing power of Indian ritual. I was more than receptive to these stories; I was greatly moved by them. I saw them being written and was dazzled by them. They were among my first literary experiences, together with a roughly done country *Ramlila,* a pageant-play based on the Ramayana epic.

I wonder what Edgar Mittelholzer would have made of my father's story in the green-covered booklet (if in his mood of final Buddhist resolve he could have broken off to look at it). I don't think he would have made much of it. Edgar's greatest wish was to be a popular writer in the style of the 1930s or even earlier, and, amazingly, he half succeeded. Just as house-brokers talk of situation, situation, situation, so Edgar believed in story, story, story (he actually used these words to me once). He also with his uncertain Dutch-Swiss-Guyanese past had his own idea of what was universal. He would have seen my father's story as folklore, Indian local colour, far away, and to a certain extent he would have been right; my father should have written of the 1940s world around him and not gone back to a misty world of 1906.

Edgar, and other people who at various times have asked me about my influences, would have been puzzled by the importance I attached to those stories. They not only gave me an example of literary labour; they gave me an idea of my background and my past. I was born in the Indian countryside of Trinidad, but I very soon began to live away from it. My father's stories peopled that countryside for me, gave me a very real kind of knowledge. Without this knowledge in colonial Trinidad I would have been spiritually adrift like so many of the people around me whom I observed later. I suppose I would have been like Edgar and others, fabricating an ancestry for myself—the colonial neurosis—or even like Sam Selvon, who was Indian and handsome, but had been cut off from his background (in his stories his ignorance of Indian ways was like a kind of illiteracy), and had only the race and the good looks to show.

Perhaps my father's stories matter more to me than to anybody else. My father first brought them out in a little blue-covered booklet in 1943, rather like Walcott's *25 Poems* six years later. Walcott's book was printed by the Advocate newspaper press in Barbados, my father's by the Guardian Commercial Printery in Trinidad, the printing press of the *Trinidad Guardian*. Both books were sold for a local dollar, about twenty-one pence, at that time a labourer's daily wage. There was no great fuss made about my father's book, much less than that made for Walcott's; even in Trinidad the material was thought to be too far away. But the thousand copies that were printed were sold, mainly to Indians who, I imagine, liked reading about themselves, liked seeing Indian names in print, and liked seeing everyday Indian life given a kind of dignity. So the book was a success in 1943–44. It didn't have anything like that success later.

In 1976 André Deutsch did a volume with a long preface by me and enthusiastic jacket copy by Diana Athill. It was remaindered. Heinemann tried again, with a shorter, elegantly produced volume, in 1994. I haven't heard about it; I suppose there was nothing to report; and I haven't pressed. It was done ten years later in India. Even by the low standards of Indian publishing this was an awful job, with not a descriptive line about the text; the book might have been a book of magic, a cookbook, or a book of wise Indian sayings; the publisher said he was busy. The stories, if the publisher had had an hour to spare, might have been offered as pioneer work from the diaspora. But materialist India is materialist India, with no idea of its history or literature, and though there is now much talk of the Indian diaspora, the only diaspora Indians care about is the one through which they might get a green card or a son-in-law or daughter-in-law with American citizenship. Every Sunday, in newspapers north and south, you can see the frantic needs advertised in the classified matrimonial columns.

I have to accept now that the stories are dead and live only for me. Walcott's island was like mine, but we were worlds apart. Two important facts made for this difference. I was born in Indian Trinidad in 1932; and from about the age of seven I saw my father writing his stories. This meant that from an early age I began to inhabit a distinct mental world—distinct from the rest of the island, and distinct even from the rest of my mother's extended family. There was this further great difference between Walcott and myself. I could, when my vision grew wider, beyond our small community, comprehend his needs and yearnings (the black children freed from homeless ditties, the brown hair in the aristocracy of sea); but there are parts of me that will be a puzzle to him.

His vision of the island is not mine; and a man with Walcott's island deep in his head and heart will look at the rest of the world in his own way. He will not (to give an extreme example) be interested in Tony Powell's England, or feel sufficiently connected to it, to be able to judge the writing that comes out of it. The artificiality of P. G. Wodehouse and Agatha Christie is another matter; these writers, who seem very English, can be assessed by anyone; the books themselves are modern fairytales, a form in which for various reasons the myth-making English excel.

Tony would have liked, as part of his Englishness, that delicate and special thing, to be taken up into that myth-making scheme. After the war, towards the end of the big novel, there is a tremendous thanksgiving service in St. Paul's. The narrator attends. He hasn't actually had much of a war, but at this moment he is like Henry the Fifth after Agincourt. He quotes the whole of the original version of "God Save the King" sung at the service. This is meant, fraudulently, and rather too easily, I feel, to cast a retrospective epic quality on all that has gone before, much of which has been trivial. It was Tony's play for the English myth. It was what he expected would come to him, some recognition of him as the twentieth-century English myth-maker; and his little American success, when he was deep in the sequence, seemed to point finally in that direction. But his autobiographical novel was just that: autobiographical and private, full of particularities, appreciated best by people who knew the ins and outs of the life; and his little American success didn't last.

IT WAS FRANCIS WYNDHAM, a reader at Deutsch, who wrote to Tony Powell about me in mid-1957. Francis had been the first reader of my first book. He liked it but Deutsch wanted a novel. I provided that quite soon (the days seemed longer then) and when a year or so later it was published I met Francis with Diana Athill one morning in the new Gaggia coffee house in Dean Street, not far from the Deutsch office.

Francis had a space, rather than a room, in that office, a space so small between partition and partition that he had to ease himself in to sit at his table; and he said he was paid so little by Deutsch that if it was any less Deutsch would go to jail. I had no idea then or till much later that Francis was a man of widespread connections. It is possible that this innocence of mine made our friendship easier. I liked him for his intelligence and wit; I suppose he was the first bookman and the first true intellectual I had got to know. For some time after that first meeting we met once a week.

In due course a letter or a card came from Tony Powell. He was literary editor of *Punch* at the time, and they had done a kind review of my first book. We arranged then on the telephone to meet at El Vino. It was the journalists' bar in Fleet Street. Tony was attractive, easy to talk to. I thanked him for the kind review in *Punch*. It turned out that he had not only sent the book out for review; he had read it. This was more than I expected. He then said something which I thought very wise, and was to use many times, and finally appropriate. He said that, whatever its flaws, a writer's first novel had a lyrical quality which the writer would never again recapture. This was at a higher level of critical appreciation than I had met.

He told me that three or four years before he had also met Kingsley Amis for the first time at El Vino. This was before Amis's great success with *Lucky Jim*. Tony had liked Amis's reviews and had been moved to get in touch with him. At that first meeting Amis said he couldn't stay as long with Tony as he would have liked; he had arranged to meet, at that very place later that day, "a very foolish man." This gave a piquant touch to that first meeting, with Tony wondering who Amis's foolish man could be. In time the innocent arrived: it was Terence Kilmartin, literary editor of the *Observer,* future reviser of Scott-Moncrieff's Proust, and not a foolish man at all.

It was Amis's little joke, and it was typical of Tony to cherish it. He delighted in his friends, saw them all as special, liked as it were to walk round them, to see all sides of their character; and he did so without malice. The absence of malice was the great revelation. He kept the letters of all his friends, and could so easily pull out from his little office a John Betjeman or Constant Lambert of the 1930s (the Betjeman classical and cramped, the Lambert bold, with a broad, flat nib) I suspected his letters were filed alphabetically.

He was, it might be said, a collector of people, like the seventeenth-century "character"-writers, or the John Aubrey of *Brief Lives.* During the war he wrote a book about John Aubrey. You might have thought that the match between author and subject was perfect; but Tony's book was dull, as Graham Greene said to Tony in some exasperation one day; and Tony, who told the story in print, didn't (in this account) make a reply. You felt that the Aubrey book was a chore; and again it was strange that for a man who lived the author's life to the full so many of his books gave that impression, of being a chore. Before the war it was the labour of a man trying hard to make his way; after the war it was the labour of a man starting up again, being very careful, and anxious not to fail, until he felt he had succeeded.

I loved the Tony who was like John Aubrey, the collector of people and their oddities, the man who seldom censured, and thought that people and especially his friends made the world glamorous. Without formulating it, that breadth of vision, that kind of welcome, was one of the things I had actually been hoping to find in the larger society of England. I had longed to get away from the easy malice of the small place I grew up in, where all judgements were moralistic and hateful and corrupting, the judgements of gossip. But so far I hadn't been lucky in England. I had expected much from the university; but I had found little there. At my college they were for the most part provincial and mean and common; and it was like that at the BBC as well.

There was Henry Swanzy and, quite recently, Francis Wyndham. But these were exceptional men. And now, so soon after Francis, I had found Tony Powell. This was the England I had wanted to find, and had given up looking for. The "lyrical quality" of a first book: I had never heard any literary judgement so profound spoken so easily; there was a depth of civilization there. And there was that depth, too, in Tony's attitude to people. I consciously began to copy that; it became part of my own personality. It was the glamorous rather than moralistic thing I needed, to set against the smallness and jealousy that ruled the world. (Many years later I was to meet a successful European publisher who, as a matter of strong principle, it was said, was jealous of everyone.) But without Tony's example I would not have known what I was looking for. In time I was to find out that there was little in his books for me; but Tony was, more than he knew perhaps, an important part of my education, and part of my training as a writer.

At the time of my meeting with him the only thing I knew

of his work was a radio adaptation of *What's Become of Waring,* one of the pre-war books. It was published in 1939 and Tony would say it sold 999 copies, suggesting that its further fruitful career was scuppered by the outbreak of the war. The idea of the book was a simple one, that of a travel writer who doesn't actually travel, an idea so simple that it wouldn't be surprising to learn that it had furnished half a dozen books before and after. The narrative, such as it was, was muffled in its radio adaptation by a torrent of words. So it was in the book itself, with everything over-explained, in the Powell manner.

I couldn't say I hadn't liked the radio adaptation. So I asked Tony what he had made of it. This piece of literary guile—throwing the ball into the other man's court, as it were, useful in similar circumstances in later years—had come to me on the spur of the moment.

He said he liked it, but actors invariably over-acted. They couldn't say a simple thing like "Would you have a cigarette?" without trying to inject drama into it. And I suppose that was one of the other things that had wearied me.

IT IS AMAZING TO ME—leaving aside the radio version of *What's Become of Waring*—how often I was baffled by famous novels of the time. I didn't understand Graham Greene's *The Quiet American,* which was a hit in 1955. It was set in Indo-China and was about the war to come; it established his reputation as a man who saw things that were about to happen. I didn't understand the book partly because I didn't read the newspapers, or read them in a selective way. I didn't read

American news; I read nothing about the presidential campaigns, and pitied journalists who had to follow them. I didn't read about English politics; I had never voted. When De Quincey (like Tony Powell in his wish to collect great or unusual men) met Wordsworth he was disappointed that the great man, a poet after all, was interested in something as ordinary as a newspaper.

I wonder what an enquirer like De Quincey would have made of me. I would have said, if I was asked, that though I knew nothing about American politics I took an interest in the world. I read the *Manchester Guardian* and *The Times*. Graham Greene used to tell interviewers (it is their habit to read the previous interviews and they all then ask the same questions) that what they saw as his foresight about Vietnam and other places came from his careful reading of newspapers. My attitude to detailed newspaper-reading was different. I saw it as a form of idleness. Things ran their course; elections took place, and the United States and Great Britain continued much as they had done; to read about what was happening in the interim was a waste of time; and so, too, was to read articles about, say, the best prime minister we never had.

The virtue of this was that when I began to travel I saw places fresh. But it was the only virtue. I had longed for years to be in the great world. I was there now, but I stayed away from its affairs. I lived as I had lived in Trinidad. I had criticised others from my background for their lack of curiosity. I meant curiosity in cultural matters; but the people I criticised would have had their own view of the relative importance of things and they would have been astonished by my lack of political curiosity. As soon as I begin to examine the matter I see that this ignorance of mine (there is no other word for it), this limited view, was an aspect of our history and culture. Historically, the peasantry of the Gangetic plain were a powerless people. We were ruled by tyrants, often far off, who came and went and whose names we very often didn't know. It didn't make sense in that setting to take an interest in public affairs, if such a thing could be said to exist. What was politically true of the Gangetic plain was also true of pre-war colonial Trinidad; in this respect at any rate the people who had made the long journey by steamship from India found nothing to jolt them.

That outer world, out of our control, was oddly echoed for the children of the house in our inner world. In my grandmother's house, even when we lived in Port of Spain, there were constant religious occasions, readings from the Indian scriptures that might last for a morning or a day or two days or sometimes for a week.

Pundit Dhaniram (whom no one particularly respected) might arrive from the country on his motorbike. He was a handsome, slender man with a shining brown skin and a faraway look. His forehead was freshly marked with sandalwood paste; but apart from this he didn't look at all like a pundit. The motorbike gave him a rakish air; he might have been (like some pundits) a man who was holding down a well-paid job on one of the American bases, driving a truck for five dollars a day (ten dollars if you owned the truck). But when Dhaniram had changed into the things which he had brought in a little box strapped to the carrier of his bike, his dhoti and white tunic and beads and stylish tasselled scarf, and when he lolled on the white cotton spread that had been laid out for him, and talked wisely in his soft voice of this and that, he looked good and it sounded all right.

I didn't know Sanskrit or the Hindi of religious discourse and had (like the ancient Romans) learned to live with the idea that our religion, though personal to us, a private possession, was a mystery, conducted in a language which we children couldn't now understand, the emblems of some of its rituals at once village-like and familiar and far away: the plastered-earth altar, our version of the turf altar of the classical world, planted with a cut-down young banana tree, with the sacrificial aromatic fire of pitch-pine chips fed with clarified butter and brown sugar.

That was the half-world in the privacy of our extended family. There was another, little-known world outside, always there, always visible when you went out, and mysterious in a different way. In Trinidad we grew up with the simplest idea of society or human association: outside the family, the sugar estates, the oilfields, the government buildings. Politics at one time meant a bearded Grenadian called Tubal Uriah Buzz Butler, a Bible-crazed Negro with ideas of the racial apocalypse. He had brought about a big strike on the oilfields in 1937 (during which a black policeman had been burned alive), and he really had no idea what to do next. Politics might also mean Albert Gomes, the Portuguese fat man in Port of Spain, with his Stalin moustache, dreaming of being the leader of the three hundred thousand blacks of Trinidad.

To read, in this setting, about the court of Louis XIV (in

the "Teach Yourself History" series in order to get background for Molière and the others), or the French Revolution, or the baffling political changes of the nineteenth century in France, was to read about a fairyland. No one seemed real. What was a court? What were courtiers? What was an aristocrat? I had to make them up in my mind, though for the most part I left them as words. In this way I picked up many facts, insubstantial, hard to get a grip on, but I lived in a cloud of not-knowing, and the world around me, in my grandmother's house during its religious occasions, and in my school books, was a blur. I lived easily with this; it had come to me, strangely, with my education, my little learning; and I thought only that was how it was.

This was the lack of vision I took with me to England with my bright boy's scholarship. I had first to understand the lack and had then to read and write myself out of it.

But I feel that the writers I couldn't read were also partly to blame. If in 1955 I didn't know what *The Quiet American* was about, and had to leave the book two-thirds of the way, it was because Graham Greene hadn't made his subject clear. He had assumed that his world was the only one that mattered. He was like Flaubert in *Sentimental Education*, assuming that the complicated, clotted history of mid-nineteenth-century France was all-important and known. Not all metropolitan writers were like Flaubert and Greene, though. Maupassant in his stories, with little room to manoeuvre, but with his details of time and place always concrete, giving even minor figures a name and a family history (he always deals with a whole life), made his far-off world complete and accessible, even universal. You didn't need to know the history of nineteenth-century France to understand the awfulness of his peasants or the wounds of the Franco-Prussian War. The Russians (with the exception of Turgenev) were always clear. Mark Twain from far-away Missouri was always clear. And it seemed, in a strange way, that at the end, when the dust settled, the people who wrote as though they were at the centre of things might be revealed as the provincials.

In 1955, the year of *The Quiet American,* Evelyn Waugh published *Officers and Gentlemen,* the second volume of his war trilogy. This gave me trouble too. I felt, in spite of the usual disclaimer, that it was too close to fact. It required some knowledge of the course of the war and of a small campaign in a small place; and it was written in a mannered, flippant way. There were many lines of unattributed dialogue: you had to work back to find out who the speaker was. The mode might have been meant to be a form of understatement, but it was also a lazy carry-over from the pre-war comedies, suited to idle chatter, and not suited to the early stages of a terrible war. Above all, this book was laden with a strange vanity, not a national vanity, which would have been understandable in a book about war, but a social vanity within that, as of a man, melancholy before the war, who then in the middle of the war had found higher values: comradeship among people he recognised as his superiors. This was strangely like Kipling, and it made the work very private.

It was a relief, in a way, to understand from these books that as writer I was on my own. There is another memory from 1955, near the end of the year. It occurred to me, just before I took in the novel that Deutsch had asked for, that I should check the way of a master with dialogue. I bought a copy of *The Painted Veil* from a W. H. Smith news-stand, read some pages standing up, and soon came to the conclusion that Maugham was not a writer I could go to for instruction. Not because Maugham was bad. My material was too far away from his; it was my own; I had to adhere to it and do the best I could with it, in my own way. (And, at the risk of getting too far ahead of myself, what a relief it was when this process of learning began to be accompanied by an ability to discard, what a relief it was to feel that I need never read another letter of sweet nothings from Henry James again.)

The other side of this, being on my own, was that it meant I was trying to make my way as a writer in a place which really had no room for me, which had its own ideas of what writing was, and where, contrary to what I had thought since concrete ambition had come to me, there was no republic of letters.

It made Tony Powell's friendship all the more remarkable.

I HAD THOUGHT OF HIM as immeasurably secure. But in 1957 he was having a hard time. His reputation was high, but his books sold only seven thousand copies. They didn't give him a living. He had to have a job. That was why he worked as literary editor for *Punch*, and that was a job full of humiliation for him. *Punch* had few literary pages, perhaps only two, and the editor, Bernard Hollowood, a banal cartoonist, often said he could do the literary pages himself. Tony said that someone in the office split Hollowood's name when he spoke it and made it Hollow Wood. It is a story that tells a lot about the unhappiness of the *Punch* office.

Yet it was through Tony that at this time, 1957–58, I became a reviewer for the *New Statesman*. The *New Statesman* was by far the best weekly in England then. Its front pages were political and socialist and Labour. The arts pages, at the back, of high quality, could be anything politically. People liked the strange mixture. The *New Statesman* sold eighty thousand copies, a prodigious number for a weekly of that sort. To appear in its pages was to have a kind of reputation. Everything printed there went around the English-speaking world. When I went to India in 1962 many people, sometimes even sleeping-car attendants, were kind to me because I wrote for the *New Statesman* (the magazine was known to be a friend of India); and Satyajit Ray, the great film director, wanted to talk to me about the *Statesman* film critic.

It wasn't plain sailing, though, becoming a reviewer for the *New Statesman*. The first book I was sent, for a trial review (I think for a Shorter Notice), was *A Book of Anecdotes*, compiled by a much-loved bookman, Daniel George. It was really a book of jokes, and I didn't know what I could say about such a book. If I had to do three or four hundred words about a book like that today I would take a shortcut. I would pick out two or three of the more amusing items, write about them, and try to find something more general to say (I am not sure what) about anecdotes. I read all of the Daniel George book; what might have been pleasure became torment. Then I wrote the same little piece again and again over a couple of days. My head began to hurt. And then, because I had nothing to say, I thought I should criticise Daniel George. I did so in a heavy, undergraduate way. Finally I took what I had written to Great Turnstile and dropped it off at the *Statesman* office. Not long after, I met someone I knew from the *Sunday Express*. I asked him about Daniel George. He said George was a sweet and generous man. I began to worry that my awful little piece might be printed. I dreaded looking at the *Statesman* for the next few weeks. There was no sign of the Daniel George piece. I was glad.

I thought that was the end of the *New Statesman* and me. But there was a benevolent spirit—it must have been Tony—watching over me at Great Turnstile, urging the assistant literary editor to give me another chance. I was sent other things, an academic book about John Lyly and euphuism (which I liked), some books about Jamaica which gave me the matter for a few jokes. I began to be published, the *New Statesman* even printing some jokes I made about Jamaica ("A banana a day will keep the Jamaican away") which wouldn't pass today. Then I was moved to fiction-reviewing, once a month, for ten guineas a thousand-word column. Each column was a week's work. I did that for three years.

I was living at the time in an over-furnished, neglected attic flat in Muswell Hill. My elderly landlord and landlady had both been married before and the attic was full of their surplus furniture. A partitioned corner space in the sitting room, which was quite large, was for coal; it also had mice, bright-eyed and startled when you came upon them. The dormer window at the back overlooked a bowling green. From a house on the other side of the green there came on some evenings the sound of someone practising "When the Saints Go Marching In." Blackbirds raided the gardens all around and brought back their booty to the dormer roof. Sometimes a cherry escaped their beaks and rolled down slowly from tile to tile, and the disappointed birds squawked and scratched on the tiles with apparent rage.

I had given up a job I had taken principally to send money to my mother (her letters were only about money). I was trying in a hopeless kind of way to get going on a new book and for some reason—perhaps I felt the book was still only provisional—was writing by hand on unlined paper. It was a depressing time in that attic. Only the monthly *New Statesman* review gave me a lift. I used to go to the Muswell Hill public library on Friday, publication day, to see whether they had used my piece. There was always a slender dark-suited man in his twenties or thirties at a table in the reading room ahead of me, with the new issue of the *Statesman*, smiling with pure joy, cracking his long fingers over the opened magazine. When my turn came I looked first to see whether my piece was in. I was intensely ashamed if it was. And I took good care then not to read it or to look at the pages where it was. I held those pages together when I read the magazine. I have never got over this shyness or vanity at seeing my name in print.

After some time I began to travel, and that connection with the *New Statesman* couldn't be kept up. When after some years I settled down again I needed more than the ten guineas the *Statesman* paid. Tony got me a fiction-reviewing job on the *Daily Telegraph*. They paid thirty pounds, almost a living wage. But they had bureaucratic rules: a certain number of books had to be reviewed and the title of the book had to be mentioned in the first sentence of the section devoted to it. These rules made it hard to do a proper article, as I used to on the *Statesman*. It made novel-reviewing more like hackwork, and no one seemed to read what I wrote. The *Telegraph* didn't add to one's reputation. But thirty pounds was thirty pounds.

TONY HAD BEEN GOING ON all this time in his way, publishing a book every two or three years, doing his reviews. The *Punch* business had ended badly, but then Tony began to do the lead reviews for the *Telegraph*. The literary editor there was H. D. Ziman. He was an unremarkable writer, and he used to dictate his reviews walking up and down in the *Telegraph* office, greeting new arrivals and going on. I seem to remember a pipe as one of his props, but I am not sure and now there is no one to ask. He came from New Zealand, I believe, but apart from this he was perfectly ordinary. Tony, in his generous, people-collecting way, became fascinated by Ziman. I don't know why. He called him Z, and more than once he told me stories about Z, which he thought extraordinary but which did not stay with me. For Tony this fascination with Ziman would have cast a glamour on his association with the *Telegraph*. The books for review could have been posted to him in Somerset, but he preferred to come up to London to look at the books himself and also, I believe, to have a little of the office atmosphere.

And then an enormous piece of luck changed his life. His father died and left a fortune. It is probable that this late piece of luck, and the consequent absence of tension in his life, a new lightness, affected his writing and gave a certain skittishness to the final volumes of his autobiographical novel. His father was a military man whose prime had fallen between the two wars, when promotions were scarce; and Tony had thought all along that his father had very little money. Tony said he used to feel it was wrong when he visited his father to accept a gin at the old man's expense. Now Tony could forget people like Hollow Wood and all the Hollow Woods who had come later. He and his wife went on cultural cruises.

It was pleasant for his friends to be with this new relaxed man, to see the old melancholy drop away. Because I felt that though the English writing life had given Tony his special style, it had also made him melancholy. His contemporaries or near-contemporaries had done so much better—Waugh, Greene, Orwell, Connolly (though perhaps Connolly hadn't done so well), Betjeman, Amis. All of these people (with the exception of Greene) Tony loved in his way, loved as characters. He especially loved the wicked Waugh; and this relish for the character of each did away with whatever jealousy there might have been. In this way, too, I found him exemplary, setting me an example, preparing me for the hard road ahead.

Sometimes when he came up to London he asked me to lunch at the Travellers. He would talk about the difficulty of his book and ask for advice, without really wanting it; and often then—this was before the luck struck—I would see him grow abstracted, slightly hunched, deeply melancholy, his colour almost grey, the short hair or down on his old man's face standing upright.

I used to wonder why he wrote, why he had got started on the writing life, why he had stayed (many start, few stay), whether there was a true need. His writing didn't seem to come out of need. He seemed to have risked nothing. After the university he went into publishing; then there was the war; and after the undemanding war he returned to the world of books. Unlike Greene and Orwell and Waugh at no stage did he go to meet the world. His conviction was that his world was enough.

He might have said, though I am putting words in his mouth here, that the expatriate novel, in the hands of someone like Greene, was meretricious, the seedy foreign setting giving an easy drama to the characters. He would have said, if asked (he had thought profoundly about writing), that many great writers in the past had stayed with their society; and that was true. The Dickens who mattered had stayed in England. Tolstoy was at his best in Russia, and Balzac was at his best in France. But these writers were all pioneers, writing about what hadn't been written before. By 1930, when Tony was beginning, very little about these great European societies had been left unsaid. The societies themselves had been diminished for various reasons—war, revolution; and the world around these once unchallenged societies had grown steadily larger. A society's unspoken theme is always itself; it has an idea where it stands in the world. A diminished society couldn't be written about in the old way, of social comment.

About this society, at once diminished and over-written-about, it was proper for Waugh to do a wicked fairytale (*Decline and Fall*) and later a romance (*Brideshead Revisited*), a book of almost feminine social yearning (in essence like the young Walcott's dream of brown hair in the aristocracy of the St. Lucian sea) in which for fifty or sixty years a democratic English society has dreamed of ennoblement. That kind of fantasy was not Tony's aim. He wished to get it right, to be true to his experience, which was, really, to do it all over again. In one way easy, since the material was there to hand (he told me at the beginning of our friendship that he had trouble inventing); in another way self-defeating, since it had been done before, and books do not live if they are not original. (Like Leigh Hunt's autobiography in the nineteenth century, in which the writer appears to be ticking off the approved things he has done or seen, like someone on a Grand Tour; or like the cartoonist Osbert Lancaster's various vapid volumes of autobiography of fifty years ago, mentioned here only because they make the point, in which the writer is absolutely pleased to have nothing to add to the hallowed memoirs of famous people, and is content to be saying, "I was there too." Overliterate societies have their snares.)

Now that the name of Walcott has occurred in this chapter, it calls up others, and it seems to me (though I don't wish to make too much of it) that Tony's attitude to his world is a little like my father's attitude to his own world, though of course there can be no comparison between the worlds and the writing. My father in his early stories shut out the rest of the island; you might even say he shut out time; he did so for reasons of personal pain, but it was his mistake as a writer. It is hard to be first; but equally there are too many temptations to do the obvious. My father might have been a better writer if he had been second or third in his field, if someone had done the local colour before him, the religion and the ritual. My father then, assuming in those changed circumstances he still wished to write (a big assumption), might have seen the spread of material awaiting him, the things I wanted to find out from him, about his own life and the colonial society of the 1920s.

IT IS HARD to be the first. It is possibly harder to come near the end.

Tony, after an unadventurous bookman's life, retired to the country when he was forty-six. His life continued in its even tenor. He settled down to doing his big autobiographical novel. This meant that as a writer he would now, even more than before the war, have to spin things out of his entrails.

In this move he was like his contemporary Waugh, who, after a decade-long exposure to the world, retired to the country when he was thirty-four. For Waugh—leaving out his war experience—it was like a withdrawal from life. The modest country house, the formal staff, might have enabled him to live the life of the successful writer retired to the country, but it gave him nothing to write about, except, in the end, his own breakdown. Country life for Waugh wasn't like country life for Faulkner or the great Maupassant; there was nothing in it to feed or extend his imagination. English country life had been written about in all its social aspects; there was nothing new to discover. To live in the English countryside was to be sheltered and creatively to die.

Over-written-about societies have their difficulties for the writer. And in the modern interconnected world everything moves much faster than it did. The world has been shaken up; the centre of the world shifts. The literary vigour of nineteenth-century France might have seemed enduring; the world now hardly hears of contemporary French writing. In the 1920s Jonathan Cape published Sinclair Lewis's *Babbitt* with a glossary of what were seen as its outlandish American words and a preface by Hugh Walpole pleading for the British reader's tolerance of the book's general coarseness. Yet only thirty years later the Atlantic book traffic was nearly all the other way; and just a few years after, places that had been on the periphery, Latin America and India, at one time too far away and too unimportant, were better known. The very novelty of their material now ensured their welcome, and they were seen as sources of a kind of vigour that had gone out of English writing (which only meant that English material was now stale).

When I had started, in the mid-1950s, I had felt left out of things. It was lucky for me that in 1955 I had found André Deutsch and Diana Athill as publishers. Without them I might have languished; perhaps never got started. My material knocked me out of court; it took me years to get into Penguin. As late as 1961 the great American firm of Knopf was sending back my work unread; my foolish English agent, the chairman of Curtis Brown, had made me take my book by hand to Blanche Knopf at Claridges. It was all of eighteen years later that I established a more or less steady relationship with the house of Knopf. In the twenty-five years since I had started the world had altered its shape.

But I also feel—only now: it takes time to assess these

things—that what was good for me wasn't good for Tony. When he had begun his big autobiographical novel his material, an English middle-class upbringing, was, it might be said, of an approved kind. When, twenty-five years later, he had got to the end, the world had changed and England had changed. He was seen as old-fashioned, his material dead, belonging to a world that had been superseded.

He didn't really know what had happened. His generosity of spirit, his habit of people-collecting, and his own freedom from money worries made him blind to the changed situation. He went among his old friends as the old writer; he had no idea now what was said behind his back. Somebody told Sonia Orwell one day that in Tony's big book people were driven by the will. She made a face and seemed about to snort. And yet Tony and his wife Violet adored George Orwell; and I remember Sonia talking to Tony in her house on the Gloucester Road about the collected edition of Orwell's letters and journalism she was helping prepare for Penguin.

Malcolm Muggeridge, the journalist, was a close friend; or so I thought, from the stories Tony told about him. He had been editor of *Punch* in the early 1950s and Tony had perhaps met him there. I thought he was one of the people Tony had "collected." He used to come to stay at the Powells' in Somerset. A story was that he got up early and, writing in bed with pencil and paper, got through two or three of the week's articles before breakfast. Tony did not look down on this facility. He thought it was a distinct talent, to write intelligent and appetising and popular copy. It was shocking to me, after hearing so much in admiration from Tony about Malcolm, to find

Malcolm writing an unfriendly and ironical review of one of the later novels. Muggeridge had his finger on the pulse of things. This review would have been a sure sign that in the eyes of some Tony had, especially with the skittish later novels of the series, outstayed his literary welcome. Tony didn't immediately show his hurt; that came out a long while later.

Ziman, Tony's Z, was no longer literary editor of the *Telegraph.* His place had been taken by David Holloway, formerly of the *News Chronicle.* One morning when I went to the *Telegraph* office to collect books or deliver copy Holloway said to me, "You're a friend of Powell's, aren't you?" Holloway had a squint; it could make him look shy or malevolent. He wasn't looking shy now. When I said I was a friend he said, "What do you think of his writing?" Before I said anything he said, with something like rage, his bad eye working hard, "I would pay him to stop writing." Just like that; and yet week by week he ran Tony's lead review at the top of the page.

Those reviews were actually very good, better than Tony's fiction. They held a lifetime's thought about an extraordinary range of writers, and they were done in a straight and direct way. Tony didn't do them for the *Telegraph* money. He did them as part of the writing life; it was his idea of how the evening of a writer's days should be spent. He said it gave him something to read during the week. He did the review on Saturday morning. It was his rule never to spend more time on a review, and since it was his rule the time was always enough. To get the tone, he imagined, during the writing, that he was telling someone about the book.

I wish I could follow his rule. I found that the writing of a review (for the *New Statesman*) took longer and longer: Saturday morning, then all day Saturday, then all Sunday, much of Sunday evening, and then even Monday morning. When I discovered that the literary editor was at the press on Wednesday morning, I made the extra time fit. In the beginning I used to do a review in two or three hours, about the time it took to do an essay at the university. That seemed to me too much; and I had the false idea that I would become more fluent, become a Malcolm Muggeridge, the longer I stayed with the job. In the event it began to consume my time, being precise about small ideas, and for almost no reward. This was the main reason why (apart from the worthlessness of the job and the enervating jealousy of all those new books), as soon as I could do without the money, I gave up regular reviewing and never went back to it. If I were reviewing now I imagine it would take twice the time to do a piece as it took when I was thirty.

Bits of honour came Tony's way, enough to encourage him in his idea of being the successful writer in old age, the lion in winter. He went to dinner twice (in a distinguished large group) with Mrs. Thatcher, the prime minister, once at Downing Street. Oxford University gave him an honorary degree; and the Chancellor, Harold Macmillan, a former prime minister, spoke the eulogy in Latin. Both Macmillan and Tony would have enjoyed that piece of antique theatre, in which Tony was described as a second Menander, after the Greek playwright, about whom very little is known. By chance a short while later, in New York, I met Mr. Macmillan in the untidy waiting room or antechamber of *The Dick Cavett Show.*

Mr. Macmillan was in heavy brown tweed, with a cape; he looked monumental, but old and ill and remote. I asked him about that eulogy, and especially about Menander. What did we know about him? He made an open-palmed gesture with his big hand and said in his now-faded boom of a voice, "Fragments." This was what my books had told me too; it was the very word. So I assumed he didn't know much more than we did and with this obscure academic reference was, as it were, chancing his arm in the eulogy.

Tony had enjoyed the ceremonies connected with the honorary degree. He and his wife Violet had taken many photographs. They had especially enjoyed meeting the minor poet Philip Larkin, and Tony spoke so much about him, and with such generosity, I felt he was on the point of adding Larkin to his collection. I was glad that he didn't because soon we were to read, after Larkin's death, the most awful abuse of Tony, in Larkin's diary or in a Larkin letter after the Oxford occasion. Larkin, who was physically a gross man, and no oil painting, chose for some reason to abuse Tony for his—mostly imagined—ugliness.

Tony's generosity, his habit of reaching out to people, gave him a kind of protection. At the same time it exposed him to this kind of Larkin-like insult. One Sunday morning, when I was staying with them for the weekend, Tony and Violet had taken me to a house some distance away to meet the owner, a kind of academic-literary figure whose name I just about knew. Now, many years later, I met this man at a big dinner in London. Afterwards, muzzy with the poor wine, he said to me, "You're a friend of Tony Powell's, aren't you?" I had begun to recognise this opening; and it was strange that on these occasions I was cast as the friend. After all, this man's friendship with Tony must have preceded mine; his was the house I had been taken to many years before, when Tony was a grand name. And just as David Holloway didn't wait for a reply in the *Telegraph* office, before saying that he would pay Tony to stop writing, so now this false friend, not waiting for a reply from me, said in a drunken rhetorical way, as though addressing a meeting, "Tony Powell. The apotheosis of mediocrity." That was all that he wanted to say to me; he shuffled off directly afterwards, leaving me to feel that in his rage or jealousy—there were people who admired Tony in the old days but didn't like the idea that Tony now had money—he had used the wrong word. He didn't mean the enthronement of mediocrity; he meant perhaps the acme, the height, of mediocrity.

David Holloway was no longer the literary editor of the *Telegraph*. He had retired or died; that dull career was over. There was a new literary editor, and it was his idea that Tony's new book—no longer the novel, which had been finished some time before, but a book of literary pieces, essentially his reviews for the *Telegraph*—should be reviewed by Auberon Waugh. Now for some reason Bron Waugh detested Tony, and his review was one long insult. It was horribly unfair; but Bron didn't intend it to be fair; you felt it was something he had waited a lifetime to write. It was not at all about the literary pieces in the book, which were quite good and deserved a proper review. It was not even about Tony's novels. It was about an idea of Tony which Bron had built up from scattered aspects of the man.

There was an explosion, and above all the flying pieces Bron, who had lit the fuse, was serene and safe.

The *Sunday Telegraph*, the sister paper of the weekday paper, had run a good review of the book by an old admirer of Tony's. Tony had heard that there was going to be something "brisker" in the *Daily Telegraph*. I think it was that word "brisker" that especially angered Tony; and when people said that Tony shouldn't after all expect very good reviews from both newspapers, the daily and the Sunday, Tony simply said, "Why not?" He had been reviewing for the *Telegraph* for years and years; they owed him something.

Bron's review preyed on Tony's mind. He couldn't get over it; and perhaps that, more than anything else, was what Bron had hoped for. What did Bron have against Tony? Many people wondered; no one really knew. Bron was often critical of his father, Evelyn, but he wished no one else to be; and perhaps in some of his admiring stories Tony had overstepped the mark. But it may be that there was no reason, that Bron had simply wished to be cruel, and Tony was an easy target.

Unbalanced though he was with grief and rage, Tony's explanation of Bron's behaviour held something of his old generosity. He said, "Bron has always hated his father's friends." Casting himself still as Evelyn's friend.

But Bron, when he brought himself to talk about the matter, was as cruel as ever. He said his father, Evelyn, had no time for Tony as a writer, hardly thought of him as a writer, never ran him down but equally never spoke approvingly of him. I don't know how true this was. I was glad Tony didn't hear it.

And though both Bron and Tony are now dead, Bron's malice has pursued Tony from beyond the grave. Towards the end of his life Tony kept a journal. It was frank and open, and the first, uncensored volume really quite a good read. It gave a good idea of the man, his intelligence and generosity. But after the Bron review it was felt by various people that the publishers had been too lax in letting the journal pass unedited, that Tony in these apparently wild diary entries was exposing himself yet again to a Bron savaging. And though it was absurd for anyone to think that Bron needed an excuse to be vicious, the later volumes of the journal were accordingly cleansed of anything that would act as a red rag to the Bron bull, and came out of this detergent process perfectly banal, hardly more than a list of names. So for the best of motives Tony in these final volumes lived up to what his enemies said of him.

And a redeeming piece of Tony Powell was lost to the world.

THREE

Looking and Not Seeing: The Indian Way

I HAVE SAID that I very early became aware of different ways of seeing because I came to the metropolis from very far. Another reason may be that I don't, properly speaking, have a past that is available to me, a past I can enter into and consider; and I grieve for that lack.

I know my father and my mother, but beyond that I cannot go. My ancestry is blurred. My father's father died when my father was a baby. That is the story that has come down to me; and everything that goes back so far is only a family story, subject at some stage to romance or simple fabrication, and is to be distrusted.

My father's mother died in 1941 or 1942. I have one memory of her. She is on the Eastern Main Road in Tunapuna (eight miles or so east of Port of Spain) and walking on the narrow wood bridge over the roadside ditch to a small wood house where close relations live. Perhaps she herself lives there; I don't know; perhaps at the end of her suppliant life this is where she has come to die. My father, who has no proper house of his own, gives her no money; he hardly has enough for himself. But his mother might at least have found a remnant of family life to give her a kind of protection.

The wood house beyond the ditch is unpainted. Fierce sun and noisy rain have weathered it grey or grey-black. This is one of the colours of wood houses in the country; it comes quickly. People do not have the money for paint and do not think it is necessary.

In that grey-black house lies my grandmother's crippled brother Ranjit. He is a fixture in the darkened front bedroom that opens off the little drawing room. In my memory Ranjit is always stretched out on his bed, on his side, in a stale and sickly sweet smell, his spitting cup (always with a little water, to make it easy to clean) below the bed and within reach of his hand. He must have been handsome before his illness or accident; but now his pale face, full of pain, is deeply creased and looks like caked or dried-up mud.

I have a half-memory of my grandmother's clothes, her orhani, bodice, and long skirt, but I have no memory at all of her face. A photograph, just one, imprecise and out of focus, as though it is this woman's fate to be unknown, helps a little with the face, but only a little. It shows, imperfectly, a fatigued old woman with a big nose, someone made ugly by her unhappy life. No finer quality can be made out, no sparkle in the eye, no pleasure at being photographed; this tired old woman just looks.

This memory of my grandmother comes from the time when, at the age of nine or ten, I had begun to keep a diary, writing with pencil in a reporter's pad, and was having trouble finding things to write about. The affectation and falsity of that diary worries me to this day. I would have gone to the little grey-black house with Ranjit and the old lady in the holidays. It was one of the things we did, and I would have been so concerned as a diarist with my thoughts and feelings I don't think I would have been able to take that step back to see the pain of Ranjit and my grandmother. I wouldn't have been able to do that because no one else did. We lived as people with the idea of acceptance. My grandmother's poor life would have been seen simply as one of those things. Ranjit's wasted life was another. I never found out whether he had been crippled by an illness or in a road accident; this would have been an immense thing in the little wood house, but no one spoke about it, just as, later, no one told me when he had died. The people around me lived in their own way; they were equipped for pain. I lived in my own way, trying to do a diary, looking hard for things to say about myself, and in that search missing some of the big events around me.

Some time later I thought I should look at this diary, to see whether it held anything more about the time than was preserved in my memory. I couldn't find it. It had been swept away, destroyed; our family kept written things, but perhaps the pencil writing in the ruled reporter's pad made the boy's diary look ordinary. I was glad it didn't exist.

A crippled man near the end of his life in a darkened bedroom, an unhappy old lady near the end of her life, crossing on the wood bridge to the little grey-black house: to remember the setting only like that would have been to add a lot to my bare memory. But there was even more. Not far away, almost opposite, on the other side of the Eastern Main Road, was El Dorado Road, a name perhaps mockingly given. My grandmother's sister lived on this road in a big house in a big plot behind a high blank corrugated-iron fence. Her husband was one of the wealthiest men on the island, a founder of a big bus company, and still a partner in the concern. She was asthmatic, heavy, slow, but still a smoker; her pale skin had not been ravaged by sun and labour, and she had two beautiful daughters; in her graciousness she showed what, in other circumstances, my father's mother might have become. As children we visited this house as well, but kept it separate from the other; no one we knew sought to link the two.

My father never wrote about either, and it is to me amazing that as a writer he should have denied himself so much. As a writer he gave me much; but he also kept silent about a great deal. This silence of his matched the silences in real life; there were certain things, like my grandmother's unhappy life, and Ranjit's uselessness, that couldn't be talked about. I grieved for the past that I couldn't enter; and now here, even in a family with a writer, was how the more recent past was being wiped out.

Fifty years or so later, when more than time separated me from those memories, I found myself again on the island. I was there only for a few days, but didn't know how to spend the time. Feeling I had nothing to lose, I went looking (but in no connected way) for the houses and landscapes of the past. Railway stations had vanished, together with the toy colonial railway system. Country villages of low huts with mud walls and roofs of uneven thatch had become semi-urban settlements of brick and corrugated iron and concrete pillars.

I had been told that the big house in El Dorado Road had been sold to the Seventh-Day Adventists; but nothing I had heard prepared me for what I saw. Above the walls the house seemed to have been sliced away. The corrugated-iron roof had been taken off, completely, as though the buyers had thought the corrugated iron more valuable than the house itself, or as though they wished to speed up the already fast process of tropical decay. In the opened-up house, in what was still recognisably the drawing room and verandah, forest creepers with big heart-shaped leaves, streaky green, oddly decorative, grew tall and straight from scattered clods of earth on the dark, once-polished floor, looking for the light between the ceiling rafters.

I could see now that it had been a rich man's house, built to last. After fifty years concrete and timber, even the ceiling timber, were still as good as new. But all the people to whom the house would have meant something had died or had gone away, to Canada and the United States and Europe, in what was like a second folk migration, and the great ruin of the house was just there, with little meaning now, like a collapsed tree in an old forest, or a dry landslide in a savannah wilderness.

The little grey-black house where my grandmother and her brother Ranjit had died would have been not far away, perhaps a three-minute walk. Down the El Dorado Road to the main road; turn left there; and after twenty or thirty yards cross the road. But the little wood house wouldn't have survived; it would have become something else; and I didn't go looking for it.

THE EARLIER MIGRATION had been from India; it would have taken place between 1880 and 1917. I was born in 1932. India would have been within the memory of many adults I knew as a child. Yet I heard no talk of India. When that talk did come, eight to ten years after I was born, it came from people of the new generation, educated in the new way, and was political, about the freedom movement and the great names of that movement. The India of the freedom movement, a place in the news, seemed oddly separate from the more domestic or private India we had come from. About that private India we heard nothing.

It wasn't that as colonials we had forgotten or wished to forget where we had come from. The opposite was true. The India we had come from couldn't be forgotten. It permeated our lives. In religion, rituals, festivals, much of our sacred calendar, and even in our social ideas, India lived on, even when the language began to be forgotten. It was perhaps because of this Indian completeness that we never thought to ask people who had come from India, and whose memories would have been reasonably fresh, about the country. And when we lost this idea of completeness, and a new feeling for history drove us to wonder about the circumstances of our migration, it was too late. Many of the old people we might have asked about their lives in the other place had died; and some of us, becoming truly colonial now, fell into the ways of colonial fantasy, fabricating ancestry and a past, making up in this way for what we now felt to be our nonentity.

Our immigrants, few and poor and unprotected, had brought their language, their diet; their many-sided religion, its festivals, its social or caste distinctions; the deities for their household shrines, sometimes proper images, sometimes small smooth coloured pebbles standing (by a further leap of the imagination) for the images; the conches, gongs, and bells associated with worship; other musical instruments; book rests for their bulky holy books; wood printing blocks to stamp designs on cotton; sometimes even everyday objects, brass plates, water jars.

It would have been possible, from the objects the immigrants brought with them, and the religious rites and festivals they carried in their memory—taken together, like a folk memory—it would have been possible for the civilisation to be reconstructed, more than is possible for the Mayan or the Etruscan. So in one way it cannot be said that the immigrants brought little from India: they brought their civilisation. They could not describe it perhaps, except in those details that were available to them—the epics to which they could refer nearly all human behaviour; the complicated rituals and festivals that dramatised the year and kept their calendar separate from the other calendars of the island; and, above all, the deeply held ideas of propriety.

The immigrants lived instinctively; and that undefined instinctive life made it possible for them to travel far from home, in those days without telephone or radio or cinema, with their civilisation more or less complete. It was for that same reason that the transported civilisation, existing mainly in the mind, was fragile, liable to perish or grow faint after one or two generations. And it was for that reason as well, living with something that didn't need defining, that the immigrants brought with them so few living memories of the overwhelming country they had left behind.

Nothing about the appearance of the land came to me as a child or later. Nothing about the flatness of the plain, the huddle of the villages, the dust thick on the ground or spiralling upwards at a footstep, the long views, nothing even about the famous heat: all of this I had to experience for myself when I went there for the first time in 1962.

IN 1944 OR 1945 my mother's mother decided to have new mattresses made. We were all living in her house in Port of Spain. This was the last two or three years of our extended-family life. This kind of life was barely possible in a Port of Spain house. It was a concrete house on pillars; the bedrooms were upstairs; the dark space downstairs was a general living and cooking area, and for some also a sleeping area. The discomfort and shame of this arrangement in the town drove everyone to look for his own house; no one looked back; and that was the end of our extended family.

Before that end came my grandmother decided she wanted new mattresses made. She still had (but not for much longer) her half-feudal dependants in the country, and she sent for the mattress-maker among them. He was a thin old man. He came with his tools (tailor's scissors, principally, together with long dull-pointed metal needles, like knitting needles) and a parcel with a few clothes. A space was made for him downstairs, a little bit away from the usual scrum, where he was to work and feed and sleep until he had done his job. It was the kind of arrangement my grandmother made with some of her dependants when they came to do a particular piece of work; and I imagine (but don't really know) that board and lodge, makeshift and informal as it was, would have counted as part payment.

The mattress-maker seemed quite content. He had come from India, perhaps one of the last recruited as a contract labourer. He was a Hindi-speaker. After all these years in the island he had only a few words of English; and this now kept him insulated from the children downstairs. He worked in silence, in a cloud of fibre dust, with a dedication that I had never seen before, squatting next to a new heap of reddish coconut fibre, loosening it with his fingers, and then stuffing it into the ticking envelope, the left hand pulling at the ticking, the right hand stuffing, until at last the long metal needle was brought into play, pushing through the ticking to get the rough coconut fibre into all the little pockets where it should be, the left hand then patting where the needle had worked.

He worked in his steady, silent way, without apparent fatigue, for as long as the light permitted. That took him up to half-past five. He relaxed then, but was still as self-contained and private as before, exercising his folded-up legs, walking about under the house and at fixed intervals going out to the house yard, lean-limbed but sturdy, never going out to the pavement and the street though, as well drilled in his relaxation as in his work, talking to no one, answering only when spoken to. When he had eaten what he had been given he had a smoke, squatting on his haunches in his sleeping space, hugging his bony knees, and pulling at his cylindrical clay pipe, which was hot to the touch and at one end wrapped in a strip of cloth.

AT FIRST I had taken the mattress-maker for granted. But then, perhaps thinking of my father's mother and her brother Ranjit and remembering how much I had already missed of our past, I developed the wish to know his story. I especially wanted to hear about India. The mattress-maker was not a great talker; and language, or the absence of a common language, also lay between us. At last he understood what I wanted; but, eternally busy with his needle and ticking and coconut fibre, he was not interested. I tried to make my questions as small as possible. I asked what he remembered most about India. He thought about it for some time and said, "There was a railway station." That was all I could get out of him.

Perhaps if I knew Hindi (I had a big vocabulary but didn't know how to make phrases or sentences) he might have said more; but I don't think so. Just as (to jump ahead, to later experience and judgement) readers of novels forget as they read, so I think the mattress-maker lived and forgot. He didn't have the analytical faculty; life and the world, so to speak, constantly went in one eye and out of the other. And I feel sure it would have been the same with other old India-born people whom we failed to question about the past. India, the past, with these people, had been wiped out, just as the present, Trinidad, was being wiped out. "There was a railway station." There wouldn't have been much more to say.

Later, especially after the war, people went to India, and so at last we could get details of our private India. There was more to say about the railway stations: the cries, for instance, of the vendors of *bidis* and pan and cigarettes. But the people who brought back these stories had been made by their birth abroad, their education and travel; they could assess themselves, in a way the mattress-maker wouldn't have understood; and this gave them another way of looking. The mattress-maker's way of looking was lost; I could never understand the India he had come from.

I WAS IN INDIA when I was planning this chapter. One day I saw, in the literary pages of an important southern newspaper, a review of an autobiography of a man who in 1898 had gone out as a labourer on a five-year contract to Surinam, the Dutch territory in South America. Surinam was Dutch Guiana; Dutch Guiana was next to British Guiana; and British Guiana was culturally close to us in Trinidad. It was an extraordinary piece of luck, coming upon a book from Surinam by a contemporary of the mattress-maker, and from the same part of our private India! The same landscapes held in remote memory, the same weather, the same calendar, the same ideas of human possibility, the same languages: a little miracle, if the book was what it said it was, a little bit of the past recovered.

The title of the book was *Jeevan Prakash*, "The Light of Life": religious and high-flown and not a little vain: from my own point of view, a let-down. The author, Rahman Khan, had been born in 1874 in the United Provinces. He described himself as a Pathan, but that might have been only a matter of remote ancestry. Many of the Pathans of his childhood worked for Hindu merchants. There seems, from his book, to have been a composite Hindu-Muslim culture of the region; this composite culture has now vanished. Rahman, remarkably for a Muslim, knew Hindi very well, and was able to read the *Ramayana*, one of the two epics of India, a sacred text. Later in Surinam, long after his contract labour was over, he was still enough of a Hindi scholar, in his own account, to teach the *Ramayana* to Brahmins and pundits in the benighted Dutch plantations.

He had written his book in Hindi in the early 1940s in Surinam. He thought of himself as an Indian religious scholar, and he believed this gave him a certain standing in the Indian villages of Surinam—*And still they gazed, and still the wonder grew, / That one small head could carry all he knew.* There would have been some local and family support for his writing; but my feeling (from my knowledge of Trinidad) is that people who reverenced him for his learning and his writing might not have always wanted to read him; for these people reverence would have been enough.

I don't think his book could have had much of a circulation. It would have had far fewer readers than Walcott's 1949 book of poems. Surinam was a backward colony and its population was small, probably half the population of Trinidad. The Indian population of Surinam would have been only half the general population; and it wasn't a reading population. The book would almost certainly have faded away if it hadn't been rescued many years later by some kind of political-academic interest, concerned here as in other Caribbean colonies with promoting local culture and pride. *The Light of Life,* rescued in this way, had been translated into Dutch. This Dutch text, translated into English by some Surinam-Dutch academics and given the sensational title of *The Autobiography of an Indian Indentured Labourer,* had been published by a small Indian publisher and had made its way to the serious review pages of *The Hindu* newspaper in India. Many accidents had lengthened the life of Rahman's little book.

It is a primitive piece of book-making. It begins with a plea for forgiveness for writing an autobiography: he is only, after all, "an insignificant soul." There follows, as an introduction to his story, a history of India in fifty-five short paragraphs, each paragraph reading like a school note that Rahman might have taken down from a teacher at his school in India sixty years before or—his memory is prodigious—remembered from a basic history text book of that time: a British text book, it may be, Indian history in these notes being, principally, a list of Muslim emperors, and then a list of British governors. British rule in India is regarded as something settled. Rahman is a complete colonial, loyal always to the ruler. *The Light of Life* ends with a poem in Hindi in praise of the Dutch queen,

Wilhelmina, "Maharani Queen Wilhelmina Sahab Bahadur"; if Rahman had stayed in British India something as loyal to the British sovereign, and as fulsome, might have come from his pen.

The autobiography proper, less than two hundred pages long, comes between the fifty-five paragraphs of the history of India and a polemical fifty-page account of a childish religious dispute with a Brahmin in Surinam. It would seem, from these "fillers," that Rahman didn't feel his autobiographical material was enough for a book. And, indeed, he doesn't have a great deal to say about India outside school and family. He tells us about his family connections, his family's rich patrons, his schools; and he talks at length and very precisely about his examinations, still important to him after fifty years (this no doubt explains his lasting memory of his history lessons). He has much more to say than my grandmother's mattress-maker, but as a narrator he has something of the mattress-maker's incompleteness. He has no feeling for the physical world about him. It is quite startling to see a photograph of his school in India (provided by the book's editors); nothing in Rahman's words suggests a fine decorated brick building, as this is or was; without the photograph we would have been free to create anything we wanted. He has no sense of the passing of time, or cannot communicate it. Once he allows himself to be recruited by the Surinam agents he is moved from depot to depot; he gives no description of these depots, judging each only according to the quality of the food given out.

But his narrative tools are suited to his vision. His world is full of religious rituals, of vows made and then carried out. He deals in wonders: men who fight tigers, men who suffer from dreadful maladies and are then cured by wise healers, both the details of the maladies and the extraordinary cures clearly remembered fifty or sixty years later. For one cure a big tortoise had to be brought to Rahman's father's house. It was easy enough for a fisherman to catch a tortoise. But then the tortoise had to be made to urinate; and then the urine had to be collected and mixed with the powder of a baked earthworm. Rahman's father didn't know how to get the tortoise to urinate. But the wise and famous old hakim, who had prescribed the cure, laughed and told Rahman to bring a stove, a pan, and some firewood from his mother. Rahman did as he was told. The firewood was lighted, the pan was put upside down on the stove, and when the pan was sufficiently heated the hakim put the poor tortoise in the pan or on the pan and pressed him down with his shoe. Sure enough, in this story, the tortoise urinated, and the urine was collected in another pan. Rahman was then sent to dig for three earthworms (three: Rahman is as precise as this, fifty or sixty years later). He brings the earthworms to the hakim, who (with a similar precision, and for an unstated reason) bakes only two and a quarter on the pan. From the mixture of the urine and the baked worm three tablets were made, and the patient (an assistant to a rich Hindu landowner) was told to swallow one tablet a day.

He was cured, of course. But it did him no good. Part of the cure was that the patient should abstain from dairy products for six months. This was not easy in India, where milk and milk sweets, curds, and cottage cheese are important parts of the vegetarian diet. The patient somehow abstained. Until one day, or late one evening, when he was tired and hungry after a day's hard travel on a palanquin (carried by four men), he sent his servant to the bazaar to get something to eat. It was eleven; most of the market stalls were closed. The servant could only find a milk sweet. It cost four annas, something between a penny and twopence. The servant took it back to his famished master. The master was tempted. With the first mouthful of the delicious sweet he remembered what the hakim had said. He should have stopped, but he didn't. He ate to the end and—this is an Indian story—began to prepare for his death.

He straight away, that very night, told his overtaxed palanquin men to take him back home. When he got there he sent for the hakim. The hakim came and said he could do nothing: the eater of the milk sweet was going to die in two weeks. And then—in this Indian story—the hakim simply went away, leaving the patient to order his affairs and deal with things as best he could. Two weeks later the patient died. For Rahman this death (so accurately foretold), almost more than the earlier cure, was a proof of the gifts and splendour of the hakim.

Rahman had earlier had a personal proof of the man's talent. It was at the time when they were exercised about the tortoise urine and the three earthworms. It was a Sunday afternoon and Rahman, a boy of thirteen, was playing with some friends in the doorway of his family house. Rahman's father and the hakim were sitting in the portico. Rahman's father called him. Rahman went and sat in front of them. The hakim held Rahman's hand, considered the boy's palm and forehead, counted and assessed the lines, and prophesied the boy's future. Rahman's father was awed. To have your future told like that, by a hakim, was to be marked and blessed; and Rahman's father raised his arms to the sky and called on Allah in gratitude.

Rahman's India is full of this kind of wonder, where some men can go behind the play of events and study the workings of fate. The wonder of the seer follows the wonder of the healer; and in the background are the stupendous rituals of both religions. The effect is of an enticing, brightly coloured place where anything might happen; a man has only to let himself go. In Rahman's view of the world Satan led one astray; Allah rescued one. So the devout man was always protected, and never had to live with the consequences of his actions.

When he was seventeen, and in the middle school, in a hostel far from home, Rahman decided, with a friend of the other religion, the nephew of a temple priest, to run away. In the hostel he had to cook for himself. He hated cooking; it blighted his days; he couldn't get the peace of mind he needed to study, and he couldn't sleep properly. In this mood he went home for a five-day school break. He slept next to his father; it was their custom. He saw that his father was keeping a money-bag under his pillow; he found out that the money being guarded in this way, ninety-five rupees, was to pay the tax on his crops. About two o'clock one morning, when he thought his father was sleeping, Rahman stole the bag and went to join his friend.

There was a small Indian kingdom with its own maharaja and its own rules about fifteen miles away. That was where Rahman and his friend thought they should go. They ran seven miles without stopping and came at daybreak to a village where Rahman had relations. They had breakfast and a bath there and later, telling Rahman's relations they wanted to have a look at the village, began to walk to the maharaja's kingdom. They got there at about half-past four. It was as magical a place as they expected. There was a hill, and behind the hill a fortress wall. The maharaja's palace was at the top of the hill and had a pinnacle of gold.

The city gates were open. They went in and Rahman says they found themselves in the land of their dreams. In Rahman's brightly coloured, *Arabian Nights* world anything is possible; and it is no surprise to him or to his reader that this land of dreams is just fifteen miles away from his family house. By the maharaja's orders the city has been decorated for this month, and a fair is in full swing, with booths and sports and games and a circus. Rahman has relations in this place too; so there is a house where they can have supper (Rahman's temple friend being given flour and pulses and his own pots and pans to cook his vegetarian food) and where they can sleep. In the morning they go out to explore the golden city. There are temples, mosques, lakes, a well-stocked zoo; and there is the maharaja's palace.

Near the gate to the audience hall they find—a Rahman touch—a holy man. He is sitting on the ground and writing. They go up to him, ask his permission, and sit beside him. They tell him, when he asks them, that they come from afar and are looking for employment. In Rahman's *Arabian Nights* world problems arise only to be resolved, especially if there is a holy man about. And this holy man tells the two young men that the maharaja of the state is kind and generous to the poor. Every day at noon a cannon is fired; the maharaja can then be approached and petitioned; the sentry at the inner palace gate will stop no one.

They wait outside the gate. At noon, as the holy man said, the cannon is fired. A bell rings; and the sentry who has been walking up and down outside the gate pushes it open. Another sentry appears and leads them to the hall of audience. The young men are ready to faint at the richness of what they find: the carvings, the silver chandelier, the carpet soft and smooth, the perfume. The maharaja's high officials and courtiers, splendidly attired, sit with their hands in their laps. The young men are led to the presence area. They put their palms together, in the proper suppliant gesture, and bow their heads. When the maharaja appears—he is not described—they kneel. The maharaja asks them to rise. Rahman is stunned by the radiance of the ruler's face and the jewels of his crown.

The maharaja—who does this kind of thing every day—is brisk and matter-of-fact. He asks what his petitioners want. Rahman says he wants to earn a living. The maharaja asks whether he can read and write. When he says yes, the maharaja throws (this is the word Rahman uses) a knife and a pen without a nib (clearly a reed). He asks Rahman to make a pen; Rahman does so and puts the reed pen and the knife on the ivory table in front of him. The maharaja examines the pen, writes something on a piece of paper, and asks Rahman to write his name and address on that piece of paper. Rahman does so. The maharaja directs his secretary to make a note of Rahman's name and tells Rahman to come back on the following day at ten.

Rahman's friend, the young man from the temple, had no schooling. He was fat and sturdy, though, and the maharaja thought that a place might be found for him in the army. He too was asked to come back the next day.

So it had all been as the holy man had said. But Rahman and his friend never went back to the maharaja's palace with the pinnacle of gold and the glittering ruler. They had left too many clues with Rahman's relations in two towns; and now, unhappily for them, they were plucked from the land of dreams and taken back to what would have seemed the greyness of home. The kitchen fire was lighted there for the first time for three days. Allah was thanked, and Rahman's father fed the poor. (Always, in this account, the poor, the bearers of palanquins, perhaps, called out on these occasions from the encompassing shadows, and were religiously fed.)

IT MUST HAVE BEEN this easy escape from the school hostel to the maharaja's city and palace, his welcome by holy man and ruler, his vision of new possibility, that made Rahman ready, when the time came, to sign on for Surinam. There was another reason. His father wished now to "tie him down," to prevent him running away again, and he thought, strangely, that the best way would be by getting the young man married. So at the age of eighteen Rahman was married. He didn't raise a murmur. He gives the event half a line, and doesn't allow it to interfere with his narrative. "After the marriage ceremony and holiday I returned to school and resumed my studies in a sincere way."

In the same passive way he allows himself, six years later, when the big occasion arises, to be led to the Surinam emigrant depot. He says at first, like many Indian emigrants, that he was tricked; but the narrative shows that he was more than half willing. Somewhere in his head there would have been a memory of a palace with a golden pinnacle and a jewelled ruler.

He doesn't leave India right away. He spends more than six months in the depots in Kanpur and Calcutta. He could have gone to a magistrate and said he had changed his mind; he could have written to his father. But for six months he is content to do as he is told, to move here and there, noticing only the quality of food he gets in various places. In the middle of this period of waiting he does write to his father; but it is only to say that he is going to Calcutta, and he gives no address. Just before he boards the ship he writes again; he tells his father he is going to the "island" of Surinam.

Fifty years later he writes of his actions, "Holy Allah had picked me out and I was destined to leave Hindustan." It is his only explanation, and it fits his world view. In Rahman's brightly coloured India, Satan misleads, Allah in the end rescues. So a devout man is always safe. He has no idea where Surinam or South America is, and he really has no wish to find out. He believes that on the two-month journey by sailing ship he will never lose sight of land; this means, in effect, that he has believed that the brightly coloured land of India will always be with him; there will always be protection of some sort.

But the plantation world of Surinam is grey. There are no rituals and festivals in the background; it is like the change that occurs more than halfway through *Uncle Tom's Cabin*. In the drab plantations, the drab unpainted estate houses with rusting corrugated-iron roofs, the drab barracks, there are strange illnesses, ghosts, mysterious balls of fire; but there are also African healers. A man from India has to make the best of this new world.

My grandmother's mattress-maker had made the journey Rahman had made. He would not have had the means to tell me about India. He could think only about the biggest and most modern thing he remembered: the railway station. He would have been separate, culturally far away, from his children. He was as solitary as he appeared.

RAHMAN, WHO WAS never to lose his *Arabian Nights* idea of the world (essentially a child's idea), was born in 1874 in north-central India, a hundred miles south of the great city of Lucknow. Mohandas Gandhi, who was to change the face of India, was born in 1869, in Gujarat, seven hundred miles or so to the south-west. Gandhi was born to a view of the world that was dimmer than Rahman's, more earthy (no jewelled rulers, no palaces with golden pinnacles), though his people were much better off. He was born in a region of petty feudal states and his family were small-scale administrators of those states, moving more or less easily from one state to the other. It comes out in an aside in Gandhi's autobiography that his father earned three hundred rupees a month, about twenty-five pounds. At one stage he moved from the state of Porbandar on the coast to Rajkot in the interior, a hundred and twenty miles away, a hard journey in those days: five days on a bullock cart. (Stagecoaches in England, in the great days, just before the railways, did ten miles an hour. To go back further, to ancient Rome in 80 BC: Cicero, in his speech in defence of Sextus Roscius, speaks of fifty-six miles being done in ten hours by a relay of light carriages.)

In 1887, when he was eighteen, Gandhi finished high school in Rajkot. He went on to a college in another town. He found himself completely at sea; he couldn't even understand the lectures. The lecturers were good, he says; the trouble was that he was too "raw": meaning perhaps that he was under-read and knew very little about the world. After a very unhappy term he gave up the college and came home to Rajkot.

There was a family council. A friend of the family advised that Gandhi shouldn't persevere with college education; it wasn't going to get him far, anyway; times had changed in India, and the most he could hope for with a college diploma, if he could get it, was a small administrative job paying ninety rupees a month. What Gandhi should do, the wise friend said, was to go to England and study law. The English law examinations were notoriously easy; seventy-five to ninety per cent of the candidates always passed. The course lasted three years; the total cost would be only three or four thousand rupees; and at the end there would be a glittering barrister's life.

For some reason—he doesn't say exactly why: it couldn't

have been only to get away from the bewildering new college—the idea of England (perhaps more than the study of law) excited Gandhi. He says it made him forget his cowardice. In the hope of getting financial help for his English venture from the government he went to see the British political agent at Porbandar, and he thought it was important to get there as fast as he could. He hired a bullock cart (twenty-four miles a day) for part of the journey, and did the remainder on a camel, though he had never before ridden on a camel. Wasted labour, pointless speed: in Porbandar Gandhi had the merest word with the political agent as the agent was going up a staircase, and he told Gandhi, more or less over his shoulder, that he was not qualified to go to England to study.

Gandhi wasn't put off; and he wasn't put off later by the religious objections of some of his family and caste to his crossing the black water. And yet he had very little idea of what he was going to. He hadn't read anything about England. It filled him with distaste—his own word—to read anything not a school book. He had never read a newspaper. He had no idea of the history of India. All that he knew of his own religion was what he had seen in his family. He had listened to readings of the *Ramayana*. From a family maid he had learned the virtue of repeating the name of Rama. He knew a few moralistic Gujarati plays. On certain festival days he had heard the Gita read aloud, but it had made no great impression on him. It is hard in India today, in a time of television and cinema and newspapers and constant political debate, to enter a mind so culturally denuded as Gandhi's was in 1887; nearly every apparently promising cultural beginning ends in a blank.

And yet he was in a fever to go to England. He rode over every caste obstacle. In his enthusiasm and blindness at this stage he was like Rahman eleven years later, in 1898, obstinate in his wish to go to Surinam (though Rahman fudges an important part of his story here, losing seven years, saying only of his Surinam passion, the many months in the disagreeable depots in Kanpur and Fyzabad, that he had signed up because he was bored by the routine of his life).

The comparison of Rahman with Gandhi can't be pushed too far, though both men appear at this stage to be untutored country boys seeking to make their way. In 1891 the seventeen-year-old Rahman, at the end of his simple schooling, is happy to be offered a job as a primary-school teacher for nine rupees a month (about twelve shillings). Gandhi, with state administrators in his background, and a father earning three hundred rupees a month, would never have been content with nine rupees. And yet Rahman was the vainer of the two. He was full of the idea of his religious learning, his knowledge (though a Muslim) of the *Ramayana* of India; he felt himself to be the equal of a Brahmin. He never in the course of his long life went beyond this little learning; and he sank without unhappiness into the Surinam bush, cherishing his village glory to the end.

Gandhi was the opposite of vain. His journeys out of India, first to England and then to South Africa, made him see that he had everything to learn. It was the basis of his great achievement.

Gandhi was fifty-five when he began dictating his autobiography in weekly instalments, one short chapter a week, for his magazine *Navajivan*. He was dictating, in Gujarati, to his trusted secretary and translator into English, Mahadev Desai, who also took part in many of Gandhi's political campaigns. Writer and translator couldn't have been closer; in its English translation the book sings, and for the first seventy or so chapters the writer is sufficiently far away from the events he is describing for the matter to be well sifted in his own mind. He is direct and wonderfully simple; the narrative is ordered. These early chapters have the quality of a fairytale, and it is possible while reading them to forget that the writer is a full-time politician, the creator of a movement unlike any other in India, and often uncertain of the next turn to take. Halfway through the book, in his account of events in South Africa, there is a narrative fracture; the politician and lawyer, the writer of letters and petitions, swamps the storyteller. It isn't only that he has already written a book about South Africa; it is also that as he is dictating his weekly instalments he begins to be overtaken by political events around him in India. It spoils the book, but Gandhi was not concerned with literature; and there is enough of the magical early part for the book to be considered a masterpiece.

I have read the book many times, and at each reading I see something new. The early narrative is so easy and beguiling that one can read too fast; and as with a certain kind of appetising fiction, one can gobble up details, forgetting them as one reads, or not remembering all. As a child, when parts of the book were read to me, I saw the painful fairytale, at a time when Indian independence was still some years away. In my thirties, when India was independent and Gandhi himself long dead, I could read the book as a book. I saw its strange deficiencies: the absence of landscape, the extraordinarily narrow view of England and London in 1888–91: no attempt to describe the great city that must surely have overwhelmed the young man from Rajkot, no theatres or music halls, everything disappearing in his quest for vegetarian food and in his wish to stay faithful to the three vows he had made to his mother before leaving Rajkot: no meat, no alcohol, no women.

Everyone who has read about Gandhi's three years in London knows about his dancing lessons, his violin lessons (to help him "hear" the music for his dancing classes), his buying of a violin (one absurdity leading to the other), and his wish, with the help of *Bell's Standard Elocutionist,* with its extraordinary line illustrations of oratorical gestures, to master the art of public speaking. *Bell,* he says, making a little joke, rang an alarm for him. He abandoned his elocution lessons (he had paid a guinea down for three lessons, and he had had two). He took back the violin to the shop, gave up his violin lessons (the woman teacher approved of the giving up) and his dancing lessons. (*Bell* was one of the books in my father's little library; perhaps, missing Gandhi's point, he had been guided to it by Gandhi's autobiography.)

London, though, was much more than this kind of frivolity for Gandhi. He couldn't forget that his brother was paying for everything, and he was a diligent student, prompted in that by the same moral sense that kept him obsessed by the vows he had made to his mother. The law exams could have been done after a few months of selective study. He thought it would have been fraudulent for him to do so; the law books had cost him much money. The logic is strange; but he decided to read all the books. He read through the common law of England in nine hard months; and he thought he should read Roman law in Latin.

One forgets as one reads, Gandhi's narrative is so beguiling. I had remembered the awkwardness, the shyness of the young man in England. The revelation for me in this last reading was Gandhi the diligent law student, reading Justinian in Latin, avoiding short cuts for moral reasons. It explains his emphasis later on law and procedure. All through the autobiography there are clues to Gandhi's later behaviour.

THE INDIAN NATIONAL CONGRESS met in Kanpur in 1925. Gandhi would have been deep in his autobiography at this time; and by an extraordinary chance we have a literary witness of the Congress occasion. Aldous Huxley was thirty-one, and full of energy (he had promised his publishers two books a year). In 1925 he was for a while in India, doing a round-the-world journal for *Jesting Pilate*, published in 1926. He was a London intellectual—belonging, in his own words, "to that impecunious but dignified section of the upper middle class which is in the habit of putting on dress-clothes to eat"—and he was travelling fast, travelling and writing, doing the famous sights, and, more or less successfully, working up new ideas about them, never taking the name of Kipling. Still, it is unexpected finding him here in awful Kanpur, at this Congress meeting, some years before the Indian freedom movement and the mahatma became well known internationally. Perhaps

Forster's *A Passage to India*, published the previous year, though an entirely different kind of book, had put ideas in his head.

There were about eight thousand people at the Kanpur Congress. They were in a tent about a hundred yards long and sixty yards wide, with a light roof of brown canvas, and they were all seated on matting on the ground. Whereas earlier in the century (according to Nehru) there would have been delegates in morning coat and striped trousers, now they were all in Indian dress and many were wearing the boat-shaped white cotton cap which was already known as the Gandhi cap. The meeting went on for three days, six hours the first day, seven hours the second, and finally nine hours, speeches all the time, and no food.

Huxley, though very young, was treated with great regard. Some people might have thought he was Professor Huxley; this had happened before in India. He was given a place on the platform, which would have been raised in some way so that speakers could be seen. But even on the platform people sat on the floor; and at the end of the last, nine-hour day Huxley (immensely tall, to add to his troubles) was all but dead of fatigue. But he had had a very clear view of Gandhi, one of the main speakers; and his brisk but sharp pen portrait of the mahatma (still little known abroad) was one that would be followed by later writers: the small emaciated man, with a shawl over his naked shoulders, the shaved head, the big ears, the "rather foxy" features, the easy laugh.

He was talking about the position of Indians in South Africa, but to Huxley's surprise there had been no great welcoming applause for him and no respectful hush while he spoke. People talked and fidgeted all the time; some called for water; some got up and went outside and came back again. Huxley, as a traveller too concerned with interpreting the externals of things, had not thought to provide himself with a translator (which would have been easy), and so we have no account from him of what Gandhi said.

The Gandhi who had presented himself to Huxley and the Kanpur Congress was iconic (the word can't be avoided) and complete, someone who might have been thought to be perfectly Indian, always there. But the emaciated small man in a dhoti with a shawl over his bare shoulders was a creation; he had been created step by step, personal experiment by personal experiment—in London, South Africa, and India—over thirty years; and the book he was dictating in these weeks to his secretary Mahadev Desai, *The Story of My Experiments with Truth,* one small chapter a week, was the story of that creation. Huxley would not have known anything of that work, which was appearing in a small-circulation Indian weekly the mahatma had founded. And yet, with his interest in mysticism and spirituality, Huxley could consider the externals and arrive at an original and rather fine appreciation of the figure and the Indian setting before him.

Huxley saw a lot. The Kanpur occasion—which should have been solemn, and yet wasn't, with delegates chatting and moving about while their great man spoke about the pain of South Africa—put him in mind of the Edward Lear rhyme about *an old man of Thermopylae, / Who never did anything properly.* The rhyme leads into a discussion of the apparent

Indian disorder, where too little attention is paid to appearances—where the palace is grand but the decoration casual and out of key, where the maharaja's Rolls-Royce makes its own statement, but the driver is ragged, blowing his nose in the end of the stylish long tail of his turban. Huxley doesn't mock; he doesn't stay with the simple observation. He wonders whether in India externals aren't merely allowed to be externals; which is remarkable for a man of his background in 1925.

But Gandhi, remarkably for a man of his limited origin, had long before grown to see in India what Huxley saw. In 1901 Gandhi, after eight years in South Africa, had gone back to India; he intended that return to be permanent, but it wasn't. Gandhi was thirty-two (more or less the age of Huxley of *Jesting Pilate*). The Congress was meeting that year in Calcutta; and Gandhi, young as he was, and with no Indian reputation, thought he should go there to talk about the position of Indians in South Africa (twenty-four years later this was again his subject in Kanpur: he was pertinacious). He had introductions to important people and he was given five minutes to introduce his resolution. He had developed speaking skills in South Africa; but he was horribly nervous in the great Congress with its many famous orators. He had been talking for three minutes when the bell went.

This was to warn him that he had two minutes more; but he took it to mean that he had to stop, and he stopped and sat down. He was wounded; other people had spoken for half an hour and more, and no bell had rung for them. Still, he was applauded, hands were raised, and his resolution was passed.

It was something, though in 1901 every Congress speaker was applauded and every resolution was passed.

More unsettling to him than the speech he had had to make were the "appointments" of the occasion—Mahadev Desai's old-fashioned word for the lodging arrangements and the cooking arrangements and the sanitary arrangements. In the autobiography he writes about them before he writes about the speech. He was put up in Ripon College (named after a viceroy). There were "volunteers" everywhere, to help the delegates. But neither the delegates nor the volunteers had any idea of service. The delegates, a little bit at sea, called ceaselessly for volunteers to do this and do that, and the volunteers, at sea themselves, tried to pass on the requests to other volunteers. So Ripon College rang with people calling for volunteers and giving orders and nothing happening.

It wasn't like South Africa at all. Gandhi—only thirty-two—made friends with some volunteers and tried in the short time they had together—the Congress lasted just three days—to tell them about the secret of service and what he used to do in South Africa. In his autobiography he says the volunteers were ashamed when they heard what he had to say. My feeling is that Gandhi, writing in 1925, when it was in his power to persuade people to do anything, was pitching it too strong. The Calcutta volunteers of 1901 wouldn't have understood what the young stranger from South Africa (only a five-minute man or a three-minute man in the speaking hall) was saying. They would have been bemused rather than ashamed by his attempt to instruct them; though, in the Indian way, they would have been polite.

There were other "appointments." The Tamil delegates were exceedingly fearful of pollution. They had worked out that the rules of their caste forbade them being seen cooking or eating by anyone else. Heaven knows what rites or penance they would have had to go through to undo the pollution if it had occurred; and so a windowless wicker enclosure—a "close safe," Gandhi says in his wicked way—was set up for them in the grounds of Ripon College. Within this enclosure, smoke-filled and choking, they cooked and ate and washed and by their lights were perfectly secure.

Gandhi was appalled. He had spent eight years campaigning against anti-Indian racial legislation in South Africa. It was the worst kind of let-down to find this travesty of the law of caste, as he saw it—comic and absurd, but as bad as anything he had found in South Africa—here in Calcutta, in the heart of the Congress, which was meant to show India the way ahead.

As for the other "appointments": twenty-four years later, when he was dictating the autobiography, he was still oppressed by the stink of the latrines in Ripon College. The volunteers, when he mentioned it, said the latrines were not their responsibility; that was for the sweepers. He asked for a broom and, already the complete Gandhian, he began to clean the latrines. He seems to suggest that he would have cleaned the latrines for everybody, but the rush was too great, with all the delegates, and he decided in the end to clean only for himself. The other delegates didn't mind the stench, he thought. During the night some of the delegates fouled the verandahs. In the morning he pointed out the spots to the volunteers; but again, they were not interested. Gandhi took it on himself to clean up, and he found no one willing to "share the honour" with him.

It was said of Indians in South Africa, to explain the prejudice and the legislation against them, that they lived in insanitary conditions. Gandhi was sensitive on this point. Being Gandhi, he couldn't deny what was said. But it might have been thought that in Calcutta in 1901, when he saw the dreadful latrine behaviour of the Congress delegates, he would have wondered about his cause. It would have been understandable if he had thought of washing his hands of the Indian cause in South Africa and India; if he had decided that eight years of hard public life were enough, that the people weren't worth the pain, and the time had come for him to withdraw, to stick to his law practice and live privately. But he didn't; it is his greatness.

His cause didn't shrink; it became bigger. It grew far beyond the disabilities of Indians in South Africa. He looked inwards: from South African abuse and the business of the latrines in Ripon College to the all-India problems of caste and the sweepers, which were as old as history, and explained the attitudes of delegates and volunteers. He looked hard at broken-down, static, cruel India; he took nothing for granted. He saw the cruelties done to the sacred cow and the underfed, overworked oxen—still true today: India took some of his ideas, ignored others. He became a great Indian reformer even while working against British rule; he didn't allow one thing to work against the other. And in the third strand of his extraordinary development he looked deep into himself, to his soul, his spirituality, which increasingly he saw as an expression of his social and political work.

His mother was a woman of simple rustic piety. She loved rituals and embraced all that came in the course of a year. These rituals could be arduous. Sometimes they lasted a month, sometimes months, and they came with a series of fasts and half-fasts. She did them all, and on occasion, depending on her mood, added vows and fasts of her own. She might, for instance, during the incessant rains of the monsoon, vow not to eat if she didn't see the sun. The unhappy children would watch for the rain clouds to break. If the sun peeped out, they would run to their mother with the good news. She would go outside to look for herself, but by that time the sun might have gone in again. Then she would say cheerfully, "It doesn't matter. God doesn't want me to eat today."

This story occurs on the second page of the autobiography. It contains the seed of Gandhi's later experiments with food, which were to lead to his discovery as a politician and the mahatma of the power of the fast. He was his mother's son. Contrary to a received idea, he liked his food, but it was easy for him to cut down, to do without, to push himself to the limit, to simplify and simplify.

In Johannesburg in 1903 he used to have three square meals a day, in addition to afternoon tea. But he didn't feel well. He had headaches and was using laxatives. One day he read in the paper about the formation of a No Breakfast Association in Manchester in England (in those days there seemed to have been associations or societies for everything). He liked what he read. He gave up breakfast, suffered a little, but got rid of the headaches. The constipation was more stubborn; it had to wait until a German who ran a vegetarian restaurant in Johannesburg (or someone like that: Gandhi wasn't sure) recommended *Return to Nature,* a book about earth treatment. Then, following the book, Gandhi applied poultices of wet clean earth (spread on linen) on his stomach at night; and was cured.

His ascetic ideas drew from many sources. He went to jail for the first time in 1908; this was in Johannesburg. Africans and Indians were not given tea or coffee and their last meal in jail had to be finished before sunset. This was hard, but Gandhi grew to think it was something he might add to his own daily discipline. Prisoners could use salt to season their food, but nothing else. Gandhi, pushing at the laws, as always, asked the jail medical officer for curry powder and also to be allowed to put salt in the food while it was cooking. (He knew, or had found out, the form: he knew who to ask.) The officer refused. He said, "You are not here for satisfying your palate." Gandhi played with that idea, of not satisfying the palate, and was pleased with it. When he left jail he adopted two of the jail restrictions: eating dinner before sunset, and doing without tea and coffee.

Later in South Africa he founded a commune and called it Tolstoy Farm. At the farm in 1912 he and his German friend Kallenbach gave up milk. (Kallenbach, a seeker after spirituality, was entirely under Gandhi's thumb. Gandhi, holy man and commune-leader as he had become, had begun to radiate a great personal authority. Two years later, in 1914, when they had left South Africa and were going to England, sharing a cabin, Gandhi and Kallenbach began to talk about the simple life. During this discussion Gandhi took Kallenbach's cherished binoculars and threw them through the porthole into the sea.) At Tolstoy Farm, Gandhi used his authority to make everyone vegetarian. Having done that, he pushed a little harder: he decided on a pure fruit diet, the fruit being the cheapest possible, so that they could live like the very poor.

It was with clothes as it was with food. He wished now to more than simplify, to dress like the very poor, whom he represented and who had given him his authority. He had begun in South Africa, wearing a shirt, a dhoti, a white cloak, and scarf, all of cheap Indian mill cloth. He wore that in England in 1914. In India in 1915, because he intended to travel third class on the railways, he got rid of the cloak and the scarf as being too showy.

He became at last as Huxley saw him ten years later in Kanpur, and Huxley would not have known what a complicated journey the small man with the shawl over his bare shoulders had made. He had drawn from many sources, some of them very strange—not only Ruskin and Tolstoy and Thoreau, but also his mother's rustic religious ideas, the No Breakfast Association of Manchester, and the South African jail code. He had created his own idea of spirituality and holy living. He hadn't stamped something out from the Indian pattern: the long hair, the saffron robe, the sandalwood caste-marks.

GANDHI WENT TO South Africa in 1893, five or six months before he was twenty-four; and he left in 1914. It is possible that if he had not spent all those years in middle life in South Africa many of the spiritual and political developments that led to the mahatmahood would not have come to him. His three earlier years in London as a law student, from 1888 to 1891, had in the main taught him thrift. He was confirmed in his old ideas and was changed in no important way. When he went back to India he was as gauche and tongue-tied as before. He found himself unable to speak in the Bombay court when at last he got a petty, thirty-rupee case; and he decided, with his unhappy brother, who had paid for the three years in London, that his best bet as a lawyer would be to go back to Rajkot and draft applications and memorials.

South Africa overwhelmed him. He had read very little; he hardly knew the history of India. He was unprepared for the racial insults and the racial legislation of South Africa; they taught him in the most brutal way about the political shape of the world, and his unprotected place as an Indian in the general scheme. In India he had picked up a few ideas about British rule; but they were simple ideas; they did not undermine him or (except in one case) wound him. In South Africa he was assailed in the core of his being; he found himself in a kind of political quicksand, which was also like a spiritual quicksand. If he didn't act he was going to sink.

Overnight, then, he became a doer; he lost his shyness; shyness was like a luxury from another life. He became a true lawyer; the law indicated how in this bad situation he might best act. He became a drafter and organizer of petitions, real petitions now, about people's lives, and not the petty memorials he had been writing in Rajkot as a country lawyer just a few months before. If he had been a little more evolved, a little more used to the ways of the world, a little more like the Gujarati merchants who had asked him to come to South Africa, his ideas might have been more like theirs. They said simply that this was how it was in South Africa; one had to work around the law and live with the bad manners, find the areas of privacy, keep one's head down and make money. But Gandhi was a country boy, in spite of the years in London. He was raw; his nerves were raw; he wasn't clever enough or experienced enough to adapt.

The theme of rebellion is one of the great themes of Western European literature. The true modern novel arises when the rebel, the man apart, feels himself strong enough to take on the established order, and when that order is fluid enough and secure enough to make room for him. At the very end of *Old Goriot*, Balzac's great novel of ambition and failure, Rastignac climbs the hill at evening above the cemetery of Paris, looks down at the "hive" of the famous city, now twinkling with lights, and declares war on it. It is a false declaration; even as Rastignac makes his vow, he can taste the honey of the hive on his lips. He wishes to possess the city.

Gandhi's rebellion is not at all like Rastignac's. He has no idea of the unbearable beauty of the hostile city. Gandhi in South Africa has small, manageable, political aims. (He is particular about that: he likes his petitions to be concrete and precise, without rhetoric, and about a specified small matter.) But then, as Gandhi's vision widens, the nature of his rebellion grows. His politics becomes indistinguishable from his spirituality. There has never been any taste of honey on his lips.

If Gandhi's journey can be compared with anyone else's, it is with that of another Indian, the Buddha. Both these men make wounding journeys. Gandhi leaves his secure small-town life to travel first to England, which is all right, but then to South Africa, which changes his life. The Buddha, a prince, leaves his cosseted palace life to explore the town outside. He discovers sickness, old age, and death. These are the things from which by his father's orders he has been shielded all his life. He sets himself to meditate on the fact of pain, and he does so until he has an illumination.

The Buddha's journey is more overtly spiritual than Gandhi's, but Gandhi's political cause in time acquires a spiritual tinge; and Gandhi's journey is more human and understandable. His political achievement is immense. He raised consciousness about caste and made possible the reforms that were carried out in India after independence; he failed completely in the matter of cruelty to animals, but that nastiness runs deep in humankind. The Buddha's illumination is opaque; it is so in Ananda Coomaraswamy's sympathetic exposition (published, it should be said, in the last year of Coomaraswamy's life); and it is so again in the book of another sympathetic religious scholar, Trevor Ling.

I am attracted to the Buddha story, and I would like to understand. There are times when the repetitive Buddhist scriptures make me feel that I do understand this great story of India, where the mysterious faith, for reasons I cannot fathom, ruled for a thousand years. But after a while I know, with these Buddhist scriptures, as with the poetry of William Blake (giving this just as an example of something attractive and baffling), I have failed again. Between the basic, beautiful story of the prince, his discovery of human pain, and his renunciation, and the complicated, even top-heavy theology of the organised faith, I can see no clear link.

Everything about Gandhi is clear, even when wilful and irritating. A certain amount is even funny.

NEHRU, IN HIS AUTOBIOGRAPHY, published in 1936, shows us Gandhi in close-up. Nehru's autobiography, once it gets going politically, is done year by year; his method suggests a man working from end-of-the-year notes. This gives the book its vividness. Nehru was twenty years younger than Gandhi. It was late in 1916 that he saw the older man for the first time and then (though he knew about his work for Indians in South Africa) he thought him distant and unpolitical, not interested in the Congress or Indian politics. Nehru was wrong. The politics Gandhi wasn't interested in was the formal politics of the Congress at that time. And, in fact, when Nehru saw him, Gandhi, though without a populist Indian reputation, was on the point of injecting himself successfully into an Indian peasant movement. It was not an easy thing to do, and after this Nehru's attitude changed. He began to see in Gandhi the authority people had seen in him in South Africa.

His physical description of Gandhi at this stage is fascinating. It complements Huxley's portrait of a few years later. It shows the steel that was in the bare-backed sage or saint. The eyes were mild and "deep," bright with energy and determination. He was humble but precise and hard, soft-spoken but "terribly earnest," not ready to take no for an answer. His speech could develop a "dictatorial" vein, and people who were uncertain about his methods, but yet wished to be with him, could be frightened after he spoke.

In Nehru's annalistic narrative Gandhi develops, from event to event, and each development is minutely noted; and Nehru's attitude also changes. He is a logical, educated man, and he can be critical, bewildered by the Gandhian way of starting and stopping a great movement on an apparent whim (at least one important idea came to Gandhi in a half-dream); but always at bottom Nehru is adoring; always at bottom there is the feeling—and it is like a belief in magic (which is part of Gandhi's hold on the enormous, varied country)—that the mahatma with his saint-like illogicality knows the way ahead, and without him, without this man who is in tune with the peasant soul of India, they have no true following and are lost.

Halfway through his book Nehru, always seeking to understand the Gandhi enigma, and his own attraction to the mahatma, arrives at the idea that Gandhi is really a peasant but on a heroic scale. He has some of the peasant's limitations, the lack of the aesthetic sense, for example: Nehru says that Gandhi, faced with the Taj Mahal, would have thought more of the forced labour that had gone to its building. But always in his essence Gandhi is infinitely more than a peasant; he has intellect, vision, an ability to attract; and his asceticism is real; his suppressed passions run naturally to spirituality.

Nehru came of an educated and rich family. He himself was educated for seven years in England, at Harrow and at Cambridge. He should in those years have been granted the gift of vision and, as an Indian in England in a high imperialist time, an oddity, he should have learned something of the art of self-assessment. Yet, going by the autobiography, he was at the end of this period a perfect blank. He has very little to report about London or Harrow or Cambridge; much less, in fact, than Gandhi has to say about London twenty-five years before. In Nehru's account these places are just their names. It is very strange.

When, in the autobiography, he leaves England behind and, roughly seven years later, begins to write his year-by-year story about his entry into Indian politics (based perhaps on old notes) he is very full; his sensibility is developed; he has a feeling for the material world and has a descriptive gift. It might be that in the beginning he is following an idea of good manners that it is wrong to thrust oneself forward. This permits him to write about a holiday skiing mishap but about very little else. It might be that his sensibility at Harrow and Cambridge was limited; it might be that in those days he was fearful as an Indian of considering himself, and thought that it was enough to take the names of famous places.

It might be that, in spite of the differences between them, he too had to make a journey like Gandhi's, from not seeing to seeing. Gandhi's journey began rudely in South Africa in 1893. Nehru's journey began by chance in 1920, with his discovery of the country poor, overwhelming in numbers, but whom perhaps for that very reason people like himself had always taken for granted: people there, in the background. In those days, Nehru says, the British-owned newspapers hardly reported on Indian politics; and the Indian newspapers, modelling themselves on the British, had little in their columns about Indian rural politics. So it happened in 1919–20 that a spontaneous unprotected peasant movement erupted and spread in the United Provinces, near Nehru's home town of Allahabad. And if two hundred of the desperate peasants, ragged and starving, hadn't thought one day of walking the fifty miles from their villages to Allahabad, to put their case to public figures they had heard about, Nehru (the son of a famous lawyer and politician) would not have known about their movement, and his life might have taken a different course.

Nehru had known about the poor of India, had seen them in their thousands at religious fairs, part of the pageant of India. But now he was inexpressibly moved to be taken to their villages, to see this pathetic domestic side of the very poor. His visit was casual, an accident. But for the villagers it was everything; they were full of enthusiasm. They called out the neighbouring villages for him, shouting "*Sita Ram*" and getting the same answering call from village after village. They all had unbounded faith in his ability to do something for them. And because he had known so little about them they filled him with sorrow and shame. As a politician he would almost certainly have become involved with the peasants when the time came. But it would have been in a more formal way; the encounter then wouldn't have had this intimate, unexpected, emotional side.

He stayed for three days with the peasants that first time. Later he went back and found that for this visit the peasants had built roads for him. He had taken a "light car" (the date is

1920), and when it got bogged down the peasants simply lifted it out. He ate with the peasants and slept in their huts. Everything would have been new to him. He would have noted a hundred details. He wouldn't have been able to take anything for granted. He would have learned to look. His sensibility would have widened, with his compassion and his political growth; it was with these peasants that he lost his shyness about talking in public, even in front of ten thousand people; and later, when he came to write, this developed sensibility would show. He would be able, for instance, to describe his jail cells in gripping detail; he would be able to do the more difficult thing of describing the ever-changing mahatma, understanding at the end that the man who was truly a great soul was also in a part of his heart a great peasant.

THE AREA WHERE this peasant epiphany, this epiphany of Indian distress, came to Nehru was the area known to the author of *Jeevan Prakash* twenty-two years or so before when he was thinking of migrating as an indentured servant to the South American Dutch colony of Surinam. For many months at that time the young Rahman had been moved from depot to recruiting depot in the Kanpur-Fyzabad area and had preferred not to write to his family, who might have been able to have his indenture agreement annulled. There is no hint in Rahman's autobiography of distress of the kind that moved Nehru. The big men in his book are landowners; they employ Pathan assistants; Rahman, full of the excitement of religious festivals and magic and magical healers, seems to think that all this is in order. Rahman's world is complete and full; we can never imagine it challenged or disturbed by peasant agitation. He never takes us off the road to a village in the interior; so we have no idea how the poor live. All we know about travel and local roads is that big landowners move about in a palanquin carried by four men, who are apparently always just there, waiting to be hired.

Rahman, whatever family or personal secrets were buried in his heart, would have taken to Surinam an idea of India as a perfect place. That idea, of the good place that was his, to which he might return if he had to, would have supported him all his life. A fair number of indentured emigrants, when they had served out their five-year term, did go back to India (this return was provided for in their indenture agreement); and many of them ended badly, frightened of what they saw when they went back, never getting beyond the docks of Calcutta, and living out their days as city paupers.

Rahman was not among them. He never went back to India, though he lived very long and (from what he says or suggests) had the money to get out of any mess. Perhaps some deep-buried idea of the reality that would have awaited him kept him from going back, something beyond the memory of the gorgeous fairs and festivals, and the maharaja's palace, and the magical healers of home with their wonderful remedies (tortoise urine mixed together with two or three baked earthworms): things far grander and more mysterious than the drab, flat estates of Surinam, where the plantation houses matched the fields and were petty and poorly built (rusty corrugated-iron roofs, grey weathered boards), where the local African witchdoctors knew only what they knew, and where from time to time ghostly balls of fire rolled over the Dutch-built dykes.

Some idea of India as a vanished perfection might have been with my grandmother's mattress-maker as well. For him, in 1944 or 1945, India was beyond reach, more than it was for Rahman; and it was easy for this unreachable India of fading memory to be turned to myth. What was true for the mattress-maker was true for the generation that came immediately afterward, my mother's generation. This generation reverenced India. There was nothing political in this reverence; the great names of the independence movement were known, but only as half-deified names; there was no knowledge of the course of the independence movement, and no knowledge of Indian art or history. Indian culture was the Indian cinema and what survived of the religion and the religious festivals. In some patriotic Indian houses I knew—which would have thought it too crude for words to put up pictures of Hollywood actors—there were framed photographs of Indian film stars. Visitors from India were adored. There was something pure and grand about anything or anyone that came from the far-away sacred land.

This adoration, this idea of India as a land of myth, lasted while India was beyond reach. After the Second World War travel became easier. You could travel the well-worn path to England and from there you could go on by steamer or by plane to India. As soon as a few people had done this India became something else. It became a place that, for the first time for sixty or seventy years, people among us could see in the clear light of day.

This way of looking didn't come to everyone at the same time. Some of my mother's sisters went to India. They would have gone to see their father's family in the distressed Gorakhpur area. They had that address by heart: the name of the village, the name of the *thana*, the name of the district: the names were like lines of poetry—they would no doubt have sung in that way in my grandfather's head, and been enough of a guide, in all the frightening vastness of India, to home. In my grandmother's house the lines were known, as a kind of claim on the great land, which not everyone in the community was privileged to have.

So my mother's sisters, the proud travellers to India, would have known where to go. They also thought it would be a good idea to use this once-in-a-lifetime opportunity to change their local jewellery, made from the gold of Guiana, for jewellery made with proper Indian gold. They did so, and when many weeks later they came back and went to local jewellers with their good news, they found that their Guiana gold had been horribly diluted. The story made the rounds. The India of their father still stood high, but the India they had been to took a knock.

Little by little the India of myth was chipped away, and India became a place of destitution from which we were lucky to have got away. I went myself when I was twenty-nine. I went from England; at that time I was eleven years out of Trinidad. And still I went to that second India, the India from which we had had to get away, and not to the India of independence and the great names of the independence movement. I went with jangling nerves, which became worse the closer the ship got to Bombay.

With all that, unavoidably, the idea of the ancestral land was with me. The water in the harbour had the usual harbour litter, orange peel, a fine web of seemingly dusty, semi-iridescent scum hung with small leaves and bits of twig. It made me think of classical lands and of people making long journeys in ancient times to famous cities, to study rhetoric or philosophy or to put a question to the local oracle. The harbour water would always have been like this, ordinary, unremarkable, until it had been left behind on the journey out.

At the end of that hard year in India, after one or two false beginnings, and after a long period of doubt, I wrote my book which, when it did come, came very fast.

My mother never read anything I wrote. She took it all on trust. And when, fifteen years after my own journey, she thought she should go to India (holding fast to her Guiana gold), it was without any knowledge of what I had gone through or done.

She came in due course to what had been her father's district, and had become the last line of the address-poem the family all carried in their head. After the district—flat as a board, coated all over with dust, with very long views in which it would have been easy to get lost—came the *thana*, and after the *thana* the village, romantically named: "Mahadeo Dubeka."

There they all fell on her, the relations of eighty or a hundred years before. They were now well trained in welcoming these people from far away claiming kinship. They offered a chair or a stool. They offered food, but my mother was sufficiently far away from India to be nervous of food in that crowded village: food there would have been like the gold of India to someone who possessed Guiana gold.

If she wouldn't have food with them, they said, three or four speaking at the same time, and all clearly relieved that no food was to be offered, she would at least have tea. And my mother, thinking it a safe substitute, said yes, she would have tea. There was a kind of flurry in the background, excited hushed voices, and in the meantime conversation about ancient family matters and my mother's journey was made with my mother, who was thinking all the time about the tea and was not on her best form.

The tea at length appeared, a murky dark colour, in a small white china cup. The lady offering the cup, for the greater courtesy and the better show, wiped the side of the cup with the palm of her hand. And then someone from these relations of a hundred years before remembered that sugar had to be offered with tea. My mother said it didn't matter. But the grey grains of sugar came on somebody's palm and were slid from the palm into the tea. And that person, courteous to the end, began to stir the sugar with her finger.

This was where my mother ended her journal entry about her visit to her father's ancestral village. She ended in mid-sentence, unable to face that sugar-stirring finger in the cup of tea. The land of myth, of a perfection that at one time had seemed vanished and unreachable, had robbed her of words.

FOUR

Disparate Ways

FLAUBERT AND *SALAMMBÔ*

FIRST IN SCHOOL you have English Composition, maybe a page or two in an exercise book, with perhaps an occasional piece of précis running to half a page; and then many years later, in a graver place, you have Essays, literary pieces, of many foolscap pages. The pen runs along the ruled page, with hardly a correction. This can give an illusion of maturity and power. But you may not find it easy to move from those essays, full of required reading, full of other men's ideas and language, to what you may already have begun to think of as proper writing, writer's writing, something personal, with authority, something you might imagine printed in a book.

That was how it happened to me. I left the university when I was twenty-two. I had five or six pounds, no more, the remnant of my scholarship money. I went to London, to a cousin's basement flat in Paddington (in a street soon to be pulled down for road improvements), and set up as a writer. It was as easy as that. Writers often say they need time. I had all the time in the world. My cousin, who honoured my ambition, was paying the bills. (He was working in a cigarette factory somewhere in the East End, and studying law, dreaming of the day when as a magistrate back home he might take money from both sides. As much as the money he liked the professional *style* of the thing. I believe he was modelling himself on some big man.)

All that my setting up as a writer required was a table, an exercise book, a pen (I would have preferred a typewriter), and a small acting talent, so that I could think of myself as a writer and stay at the table. I filled pages, writing as fast as I had done when doing my essays. I had no idea what I was doing and where I was going. I believed in my star, believed that my great ambition guaranteed a talent, and went on. Six months later—a dark time, all this period: deep down, I wasn't fooling myself—I realised I didn't know how to do this other kind of writing. If I had had even a little money I would have stopped, put an end to the unwelcome, debilitating playacting at the writing table, and looked for something else to do.

I was full of grief for some weeks, and often (especially when I was on a bus) close to tears. The idea then came to me one day, from some unsuspected source of new energy (perhaps, really, from the depth of my despair), that I should forget everything I knew or thought I knew about writing, that in anything new I might attempt I should start from scratch, seeking to do a narrative only out of simple, direct statements. This was what I did. I saved my soul and got started as a writer. For three years I stayed with the hard rules I had made for myself; and then there was no need: as a writer I was always in control, no longer hoping for magic.

I have written of this before. I repeat it here, to lead into what follows. If it is hard as a writer to make the leap from university essay-writing to writer's writing, it is many times harder for a reader—since reading is a common attainment—to arrive at a true, even a visionary, idea of a master's quality. People who think they know about prose-writing might look for a special language and rhythm. But that is only part of the story. Again, I speak for myself. It was in late middle age, after I had written many books and after I had spent some years as a novel-reviewer, that I was granted a vision of Flaubert's narrative splendour in *Madame Bovary*.

I had read an abridged version at school, and then in my twenties or thirties I had read the full text—read it in my fast, gobbling-up way. The book had made an impression. I remembered some of the details: Charles Bovary's terrible, mistaken surgery on somebody's ankle, for instance: Charles not a properly qualified doctor or surgeon, even in those days (perhaps the 1840s), only a health officer with a licence to practise medicine. Other details faded with time, as details of a novel do, but I never ceased to think of *Bovary* as a book I knew.

What did I possess of the book? There was the impression, increasingly ghostlike, of background and people, that had come to me at that first, fast reading. As a novel-reviewer I depended on that kind of impression. It told me as much as I needed to know about a writer's mind or sensibility. That was what I wished to write about in my column. And—a small technical point—I found it helped if in a review I didn't mention the names of the characters; in that way I got nearer to a book's essence; certain books condemned themselves. I had no further reviewing scheme. Other people, seeking (so to speak) to sovietise the critic's indefinable function (and to please publishers), thought a novel should be judged according to its plot, characters and style, and marks given under each of those heads. In this way all novels were "product," more or less the same, and novel-reviewing, always painful, became a vale of tears. I didn't allow that to happen to me.

Reviewing was many years behind me when I came upon *Madame Bovary* again. I was between books and I was travelling. I was in an easy, receptive mood, and one morning I found in the house where I was staying an old green-bordered Penguin Classics translation.

I opened the book near the beginning. And there, in five paragraphs at the end of the first chapter, Charles with the help or superintendence of his mother was marrying his first wife: thin, bony, forty-five, a bailiff's widow from Dieppe, in demand because she is thought to have money. To win this bride for her son, Charles's mother has had to defeat a scheming butcher. All this in five paragraphs: so much that Flaubert would have enjoyed creating, and so much that I had forgotten.

We have hardly met this first wife when—such is the pace of the opening narrative—we are introduced to the woman who will be the second wife. It happens like this. One winter night, at about eleven, when Charles and his first wife are in bed they hear a horse stopping outside the house. The maid opens the window of her attic, calls down to the street; there is a conversation; and then the maid comes down, shivering in the cold, undoes the lock and the various bolts of the front door (the effects up to this point are all of sound), and lets in the visitor. He comes into the main bedroom directly behind the maid. Charles props himself up on his pillow to see who it is; his wife, out of modesty, turns her face to the wall.

The visitor has come with a written message. It is wrapped in cloth and tucked inside his grey woollen cap and has a blue-wax seal. He takes out this precious message and hands it ceremonially to Charles. The maid holds the lamp for Charles to read. Someone has broken a leg in a farm eighteen miles away. A cross-country journey on a rainy night, and the moon not yet up: Charles's wife thinks it too dangerous for Charles on his own: better to send the stable-boy to prepare the way, and to get the farm to send a boy to meet Charles. (If Charles is only a health officer and not a real doctor, there are further gradations all the way down.)

Fully four hours later Charles starts out, rehearsing what he has learned about fractures. Little birds, their feathers fluffed out, are silent on the bare apple trees. Trees around farmhouses are dark violet. Charles, on his horse, drowses: now in his fantasy he has just left his marriage bed, now he is still a student. He sees a boy sitting on the grass next to a ditch. The boy says, "Are you the doctor?" And when Charles says yes, the boy takes up his wooden shoes and runs ahead all the way to the farm. (This, about the boy and the wooden shoes, is a magical, unexpected detail: it fixes the cross-country ride in the imagination. It is more than a rustic detail; it gives a pre-industrial edge to what has so far been a modern story.)

At the farm the boy dives into a hole in the hedge, reappears on the other side, and opens the farm gate for Charles. The farm is done in swift detail: watch dogs barking and pulling on their chains, big plough-horses in the stable feeding peaceably off new racks, a steaming dunghill with peacocks pecking at the top, carts and ploughs in a shed with their tackle discoloured by the dust floating down from the loft.

A young woman in a blue merino dress welcomes Charles at the door and takes him into the kitchen, where there is a big fire—the sun coming up, now, showing through the window—and breakfast is being cooked for the farm people: a lot of sturdy kitchen equipment here, and clothes drying in the fireplace.

The patient, the farmer with the broken leg, is upstairs. He is sweating below his blankets and—a nice curmudgeonly touch—he has thrown his nightcap to a far corner of the room. There is a carafe of brandy on a chair beside the bed. He has been using that to keep his spirits up; for twelve hours, since he sent his message to Charles, he has been cursing. Now that Charles has come he begins to groan. It is a simple fracture, without complications. Charles can deal with it. He uses a lath from the cart-shed to make splints; the maidservant tears up a sheet to make bandages; and the job is done.

Before he goes, though, he has to have something to eat; it is the farmer's courtesy. He goes down to the sitting room below: a big bed there, with a canopy of Indian cotton, and with sacks of wheat standing upright in the corners, an overflow from the store-room, which is to one side of the room, up three stone steps. At the foot of the bed there is a little table set with two silver jugs, and there Charles eats with the farmer's daughter, the woman in the blue merino dress. She is running the farm while her father is ill, and they talk easily about the patient, the weather, the frosts, the marauding wolves. Charles then goes up to say goodbye to the patient. When he comes down Charles sees the woman in blue again. She is looking out at the wintry garden, with her forehead against the window: the bean poles have blown down. She is surprised to see him. She says, "Are you looking for something?" He says he is looking for his riding crop. They both start looking.

She sees where it has fallen between the sacks of wheat and the wall and she bends down to get it; at the same time, in a reflex of courtesy, to save her the trouble, Charles reaches down for it; and so it happens that while she is bent below him his chest touches her back.

She straightens up; she is embarrassed; she hands him the crop. It is a bull's pizzle, a *nerf de bœuf*. They are both country people; the detail may not matter to them. But that intimate moment with Emma is full of meaning for Charles. It brings him back to the farm the next day, and thereafter twice a week and more. He wears black gloves and his new waistcoat for these visits and wipes his shoes on the grass before he enters the house.

When Charles's wife, the middle-aged Dieppe widow, finds out that there is a young woman at the farm, and a convent-educated woman, she is enraged. She tells Charles that for all Emma's airs and graces and the silk dresses she wears to church, Emma's grandfather was a shepherd, her father is not as well off as he seems, and there was a cousin who nearly went to the assizes on a charge of wounding. She makes Charles swear on the prayer-book that he will stay away from the farm, and the awful scene she has created ends with sobs and kisses and love. She is in control, after all; she has the money.

It happens now that the lawyer who has been looking after this money of the widow's vanishes one day, and with him goes the widow's famous fortune. (This happens in nineteenth-century novels.) Not a penny is left. There is the house, of course; the lawyer couldn't take that with him; but they find that the house has been heavily mortgaged. So in one day the widow with a fortune becomes a middle-aged pauper. Charles's father breaks a chair in his rage; he blames Charles's mother for going out of her way to arrange this marriage. Charles's wife begs Charles to protect her against the anger of his parents. But he can't. A week later, when she is hanging out clothes, she spits blood; she dies the next day, crying out, "Oh, God!" And Charles is free to woo and marry Emma.

I REMEMBERED ALMOST nothing of this carefully made and rich chapter. I suppose that on my earlier reading when I had got here I had a fair idea of the way the narrative was going and read to confirm what I thought I knew. I would have read fast to get to the substance of the book; I wouldn't have dawdled. But I found now I couldn't read fast. I wished to possess the details, to be able to recall them, before moving on. These details seemed to take me to the mind and experience of the writer. I was seeing things, light, evanescent things Flaubert himself might have seen and noted in quite different personal circumstances: the winter dawn, the boy sitting with his wooden shoes beside the ditch, the farmer's sick room with the cotton nightcap flung to a far corner of the floor, the four-poster and the upright sacks of wheat in the sitting room.

At school in 1947 and 1948 our French teacher, a serious and enthusiastic man, fresh from his own university training, had told us that Flaubert wrote carefully, concerned with the musicality of his words. I knew only little bits of Flaubert, but privately I questioned what the teacher said; I thought that prose was prose, and poetry was poetry. And I thought now that in this chapter there was no self-regarding "style" such as we had been taught about; the language was plain and clean and brief. The elegance and the drama lay in the spare, unexpected detail (the boy carrying his wooden shoes, the farmer's nightcap on the floor); this was what caught at the reader, even when he knew the drift of the narrative. The detail of Pushkin's prose stories (many of them unfinished) was as selective. But this was profounder; this was more thought-out. This was prose that had to be read slowly. I felt that to read a whole book written at this pitch of intensity would be wearing; and I was glad to find, some time later, when I read the book through, that it was not all at that intensity.

It seems quite another writer—someone coarser, steeped in nineteenth-century orientalism and melodrama—who, five years later, published *Salammbô*. *Salammbô* is a historical novel about Carthage. After *Madame Bovary* it might seem a *jeu d'esprit*. a restful piece of self-indulgence, but Flaubert had thought about this novel for many years. The wish to do a book about antiquity might have come to him when he was thirty, long before *Madame Bovary*, during his year-long travel with a friend in the Middle East. The travel excited him; he caught syphilis; he wrote scabrous, perhaps boastful letters about the brothels; they gave him his view of the countries he travelled in. But when he went back to Rouen he allowed this heady matter to go underground, so to speak. The book he began to write was *Madame Bovary*.

Flaubert said or wrote many things about his writing. He was an early self-publicist. He wished people to know that his writing didn't come easily, like Balzac's. It took time, and was original. (In this wish to comment on his own work he was a little like E. M. Forster, who wrote many different forewords to *A Passage to India* to explain the meaning of a book that hides its prompting and really has no meaning.) One of the more arresting things that Flaubert said—he said it to the Goncourts two years before *Salammbô* was published and it sounds like an early, teasing trailer for the book—was that he mentally gave a different colour to each of his books. *Bovary* was grey, *Salammbô* purple. He didn't care about narrative and character; he just did the colour. This is nonsense, but the idea of colour is interesting and must have come to Flaubert out of the labour and strain of the second book. It must have seemed to him that during the greyness of the work on *Bovary* he had been solacing himself with the thought of the purple book about Carthage to come, when he would let himself go. It gave a logic to the work he was doing, and it was a good idea for the Goncourts to play with.

Carthage was a great Mediterranean trading power. It lived by the sea and had a powerful navy. Because it had no great land area and no great population its army was an army of mercenaries. This worked well enough until Rome developed Mediterranean ambitions and came into collision with Carthage. The Romans, supreme on land, knew very little about naval warfare. They didn't even have decked ships; they learned how to build one from a Carthaginian wreck. And then they learned fast. The first war between Rome and Carthage, centred mainly on the island of Sicily, lasted for twenty-three years, from 264 to 241 BC. It ended with a Carthaginian defeat and a humiliating peace treaty.

Almost immediately then, when the Carthaginian mercenaries had been taken back to Carthage, they rebelled. They had seen their masters defeated, and they hadn't been paid for some time. This mercenary war, exceptionally brutal and cruel, lasted for three years. The mercenaries were crushed, but the war almost destroyed Carthage. It is the background to *Salammbô*.

Flaubert found the main story in the Greek historian Polybius (about 200–118 BC). The mercenary war was before Polybius's time, but he knew about military matters (even about naval tactics), and he had a good understanding of the institutions of both Carthage and Rome. He admired Rome, knew aristocratic people there, and he accompanied the Roman commander during the third and final war against Carthage in 146 BC; Polybius saw Carthage burn. As a writer he is simple and direct, with a gift of narrative; he makes complicated things easy to follow.

In Polybius the mercenary war is only an interlude between

the two great Carthaginian wars; it occupies thirty-two pages in the Loeb edition. Flaubert's novel is more than two hundred and sixty pages in the Penguin Classics. The translator, A. J. Krailsheimer, quotes Flaubert as saying, "I . . . wanted to fix a mirage by applying to Antiquity the processes of the modern novel, and I tried to be simple . . . Yes, *simple,* not sober." This is the self-publicist at work. It is obvious that to turn Polybius's spare but sufficient outline into his novel Flaubert had to pad, and pad relentlessly. He said that everything in *Salammbô* had a source; he had read two hundred books on the subject; but that doesn't make the padding less intrusive.

This is Flaubert, near the beginning of his book, speaking of the composition of the mercenary army:

> Men from every nation were there, Ligurians, Lusitanians, Balearics, Negroes, and fugitives from Rome. You could hear beside the heavy Doric dialect the Celtic syllables ringing out like battle chariots, and Ionian endings clashed with desert consonants, harsh as jackal-cries. Greeks could be recognised by their slender figures, Egyptians by their hunched shoulders, Cantabrians by their sturdy calves. Carians proudly tossed their helmet plumes, Cappadocian archers had painted great flowers on their bodies with herbal juices, and some Lydians in woman's dress wore slippers and earrings as they dined. Others who had daubed themselves ceremoniously with vermilion looked like coral statues.

Much varied research has gone into that paragraph (the languages, the jackal-cries, the Lydians painted with vermilion), and Flaubert is determined to use it all, though the paragraph could have stopped halfway, without loss, since the reader cannot in that single paragraph, and on the second page of a novel, take in all the detail and colour with which the writer is in love.

Look in Polybius for what might have prompted that paragraph, and you find—in the Loeb translation—something drier but profounder, something actually from the ancient world, more full of true concern:

> . . . One can see very clearly from all that took place what kind of dangers those who employ mercenary forces should foresee . . . as well as in what lies the great difference of character between a confused herd of barbarians and men who have been brought up in an educated, law-abiding, and civilised community . . . As they were neither all of the same nationality nor spoke the same language the camp was full of confusion and tumult . . . Indeed, such forces, when once their anger is aroused against anyone, or slander spreads among them, are not content with mere human wickedness, but end by becoming like wild beasts or men deranged, as happened in the present case . . . Some of these troops were Iberians, some Celts, some Ligurians, and some from the Balearic islands; there were a good many Greek half-breeds, mostly deserters and slaves, but the

> largest portion consisted of Libyans. It was therefore impossible to assemble them and address them as a body . . . for how could the general be expected to know all their languages?

Polybius is writing about events less than a hundred years old. He cannot be wholly detached; for him the pressures of war and mercenary armies are still the same; the situation might recur. This moral attitude gives a reality to what he writes. It might also be said that it makes him more modern. About the cruelties and general barbarism of the mercenaries Polybius writes, "Of such a condition the origin and most potent cause lies in bad manners and customs and wrong training from childhood, but there are several contributory ones, the chief of which is habitual violence and unscrupulousness on the part of those in authority over them."

Flaubert, whatever his feelings, will not go so far. For him antiquity is antiquity; he is not to judge; his duty is only to lay out what he has found. So his roster of barbarians at the beginning of his book makes only a tableau, something from the theatre. And Flaubert maintains this attitude even when, near the end, the besieged and helpless mercenaries turn to eating the dead and dying among themselves. Flaubert, it might be said, makes a meal of this horror; he lingers over it for four pages. Polybius, Flaubert's direct source here, does it in half a page, and he finds room to say that it was a fitting punishment of the mercenaries by Providence for their violation of human and divine law. Flaubert's detachment sets up a barrier between the reader and what is being described; it is theatre, far away.

In a later section of the *Histories* Polybius writes about his way of accommodating new places in his narrative. He thinks it is wrong to interrupt his story and divert attention from his theme. "Those readers who insist on such topographical digressions at every point fail to understand that they are acting like the type of gourmand at a dinner party who samples everything on the table, and so neither truly enjoys any dish . . . nor digests it well enough to derive any benefit from it afterwards." The same can be said of the laborious detail in the first hundred pages (at least) of *Salammbô*.

Gone are the brevity and the cleanness of the details from the second chapter of *Madame Bovary*, details from the writer's own mind (the winter dawn, the boy with the sabots beside the ditch, the farmer's nightcap flung far away on the floor), gossamer details opening up a landscape and a society which no work of scholarship could have provided.

Polybius, writing of things by which he is still more or less surrounded, is always simple. Flaubert is elaborate. Of the temple of Venus on Mount Eryx in Sicily, where the famous last battle of the first Carthaginian war was fought, just before the mercenaries' revolt, Polybius can write directly, like a guide book: "Eryx is a mountain near the sea on that side of Sicily which looks towards Italy . . . On its summit, which is flat, stands the temple of Venus Erycina, which is indisputably the first in wealth and general magnificence of all the Sicilian holy places." Flaubert, when he comes to do the temple or temples of Carthage (it isn't clear how many), will strain; and reader and writer will strain even more at the time of the sacrifice of the children to Moloch.

Everything now, in *Salammbô,* is big and concrete and overstated, part of the purple that lay at the back of the writer's mind during the grey days of *Bovary.* Everything no doubt comes from the two hundred books Flaubert says he read. But there is too much jewelled description, too much colour; the reader cannot take it all in, and the mass of detail actually makes for a further unsteadiness in the difficult narrative, with the writer—already like a man waiting for applause—seeming to move in and out of the nineteenth century, now close to his material, now holding it at arm's length.

THE NAME SALAMMBÔ does not occur in Polybius. Flaubert makes her the daughter of the great Carthaginian general Hamilcar Barca; and he probably has his sources. This daughter is mentioned by Polybius in a sentence but given no name. At a bad time during the mercenaries' war a Numidian chieftain comes to Carthage (Numidia the vast North African territory at the back of Carthage) to offer his services to Hamilcar. Hamilcar is moved; he offers his daughter in marriage to the Numidian if the Numidian remains loyal. That is all.

Flaubert takes this blank figure of the daughter and involves her in a sexual intrigue with the Libyan leader of the mercenary revolt. This is something he has added to the Polybius story. For more than half the novel it goes side by side with the terrible war. It is Flaubert's invention and as such it stands naked against Polybius's spare and moral narrative. Its artificiality shows. You can see the various pieces of this invention being put into place and you feel you can always see how Flaubert's mind is working. This wasn't possible in the second chapter of *Bovary*, with its constant small surprises. To see Flaubert's mind at work in *Salammbô* is not like following "the processes of the modern novel," to use Flaubert's words. It is more like seeing a writer imprisoned in a borrowed form—the theatre, the opera—and striving to do what he has seen others do.

Salammbô is a priestess or attendant in the Carthaginian temple of Tanit. She is slender (or gives that impression, which would have made her unusual in 1862) and beautiful and inscrutable. She has a python and a eunuch spiritual instructor. He has studied in many places and is full of wisdom. "Strange words sometimes escaped from him, flashing in front of Salammbô like lightning illuminating an abyss . . . 'The souls of the dead,' he said, 'are dissolved in the moon as corpses are in the earth. Their tears provide its moisture; it is a dark place full of mud, ruins, and storms . . .' " Salammbô slinks about her jewelled temple interior, never less than beautifully described, but since she has little to say it is hard to know what she feels or does or how she actually passes her days. She is a creature of bad nineteenth-century fiction, gothic, orientalist, a lay figure, meant to be seen from a distance. If she were to say too much there would be no illusion.

. . .

IT IS OUR LUCK that a religious novel, in Latin and more or less whole, has come down to us from the ancient world. The *Metamorphoses*, by the second-century Roman writer Lucius Apuleius, is better known as *The Golden Ass*, and down the centuries it has been loved for its bawdy passages; which probably helped it to survive. By a further chance Apuleius was born in Roman Africa, and was partly educated in the university of Carthage. This is four hundred years after the mercenaries' war, but enough of the older world might adhere to Apuleius to take us into the ways of old belief.

The Roman Empire is now solid; many of the famous Roman names have come and gone. Purely Egyptian Egypt has been dead for a thousand years (overrun by Persians, Greeks, and then Romans); but the Egyptian goddess Isis has been taken by the Roman army all over the empire, and her cult, absorbing other beliefs, now has the makings of a universal religion. Apuleius, with his classical education in philosophy and oratory, had also undergone an initiation, perhaps a treble initiation, into the rites of Isis; and *The Golden Ass* is about the glory of the goddess.

The hero, also named Lucius, like the author, is travelling in Thessaly. Through his infatuation with a slave girl he allows himself to become interested in black magic; the girl's mistress is a practitioner. Lucius thinks he would like, just for the experience, to be turned into an owl. But there is a confusion about the ointment, and he turns instead into an ass. The slave girl is aghast. She tells him there is an antidote: to become a man again the ass must chew roses. Those roses are hard for an ass to come by, and the rest of the novel, all but twenty pages, is made up of Lucius's adventures as an ass. They are not always funny; through them we see the underside of the Roman Empire.

Lucius is at last redeemed by the goddess Isis. She has taken pity on him. On a night of the full moon, at a particularly awful time for him, she rises out of the sea in all her majesty and shows herself to him. Thereafter she speaks to Lucius in his dreams. She makes him a man again and then she guides him through his threefold initiation into her cult. She is always radiant and joyous; after his trials Lucius doesn't like being away from her. These twenty pages about his redemption by the great goddess are humane and moving and beautiful.

As Queen Isis she is all the goddesses of the Mediterranean, worshipped in many different ways. She is Ceres, Artemis, Aphrodite, Proserpine, goddess of the underworld; she is even Belladonna, goddess of battles. She is, in fact, Nature. She makes the earth a sacred place. It is a beautiful idea of religion; and though Apuleius's Latin is strange his narrative style or manner is straightforward enough for some of his episodes to appear almost as they are, twelve hundred years later, in Boccaccio and afterwards in Chaucer.

THIS IDEA OF ancient religion was available to Flaubert. He would have known *The Golden Ass* (there are some indications in *Salammbô*), but it didn't suit his purpose, which was operatic. He wanted horror; he wanted the tableaux. He wanted the mass sacrifice of children to Moloch. He wanted Salammbô slinking about the temple of Tanit in her tight white gown and with her black python. Over the image of the goddess in the temple there is a sacred veil. It is called the "zaimph" (perhaps made up by Flaubert, perhaps not). It partakes of the power of the goddess and carries or even controls the good luck of Carthage. This bit of Flaubert's invention is of no great subtlety; it is like something in a boy's magazine or (later in the imperial period) like something from Rider Haggard or the *Wide World Magazine*. But Flaubert makes it important in the intrigue in this part of his book.

Things are going badly for the rebellious mercenaries, and it is put to their Libyan leader that he should steal the veil from the temple of Tanit. Topography and architecture, too carefully described, are always difficult in this book. We have to take the writer on trust; and the journey to the temple, which should have been difficult (with all the slaves and guards), turns out (as in a John Buchan novel) to be not so. We are there; the zaimph is taken; and then the Libyan goes to where Salammbô is sleeping. She is in white. He tells her he has the zaimph. She leans on both hands and trembles; she puts out her foot onto her ebony stool. There follows an ambiguous half-page. Was there a sexual moment between the Libyan rebel and iconoclast and the daughter of Hamilcar? Flaubert, normally so full of words, is now so discreet that we don't know.

The Libyan says, "Let us go away! . . . Or if you do not want to, I will stay . . . Drown my soul by breathing over me . . ." She says, "Let me see. Nearer! Nearer!" She might be speaking only of the zaimph; or she might be seeking to entrap him; or she might be speaking love to him. And then it is the dawn—leaving you to your own conclusions—and she is swooning on the bed cushions. The daylight restores her to herself. She calls for her servants and slaves and guards, and the Libyan makes himself scarce, wrapping himself in the veil, which no one of Carthage will want to touch, even with an arrow. Salammbô sends him on his way with religious rage. "Curses on you who robbed Tanit . . . May Gurzi, god of battles, tear you to pieces! May Matisman, god of the dead, choke you! And may the Other—who must not be named—burn you!" Protected by the veil, which is taking away the fortune of Carthage, the Libyan walks through the aroused town, and gets back safely to the mercenary camp.

The war goes on, its prospects constantly changing (Flaubert juggles a bit with Polybius's straight narrative). And then Hamilcar and Carthage are truly in trouble. The day comes when Salammbô's eunuch-protector tells her that she must go to the mercenaries' camp and recover the veil. She collapses on her ebony stool; her arms hang between her knees; and she trembles all over, like an animal about to be sacrificed. She tells the eunuch she wouldn't know what to do when she gets to the mercenary camp. He gives a strange smile and says, "You will be alone with him." She says, "Well?" He doesn't know how to be more explicit. He tells her it is the will of heaven that she should yield to the Libyan, do everything he wants; above all, she must not cry out. He makes her swear; he speaks the words, and she repeats them.

She does the fasts and the purification. On the appointed evening she is specially dressed; she touches herself with the blood of a black dog slaughtered on a winter's night in a ruined tomb (Flaubert can't resist the gothic); she is finally ready. The eunuch has arranged for a guide and horses. There are some paragraphs of description and then, quite simply, she is at the mercenary camp. She tells the sentry she wants to speak to the Libyan; she is a deserter from Carthage. The Libyan comes; they go to his tent; she sees the veil, the zaimph, resting on a bed of palm branches.

The Libyan recognises her; he speaks love to her and then (though Flaubert again isn't clear) he makes love to her. She, as though obeying the gods, yields to him; and at the same time she has the lucidity to think, "So this is the man who makes Carthage tremble." He falls asleep. She sees a dagger on a table. She has visions of blood and revenge. She takes the dagger and moves towards him. He awakens, takes his lips to her hand, and she drops the dagger. There is a commotion outside. Hamilcar's men have set part of the camp on fire. The Libyan goes to deal with this crisis, and Salammbô is alone. She takes up the veil and starts on her return. This should be difficult, but isn't: she soon finds her guide and the horses.

Carthage has the veil again; and the full tactical genius of Hamilcar (humiliated though he has been by his daughter's escapade) now comes into play. The mercenaries are horribly destroyed, imprisoned in a natural defile, starved, and then—all but ten—left to the lions and jackals (another meal for Flaubert).

The day of Carthaginian celebration coincides with the festivities for Salammbô's marriage with the Numidian chieftain. From her temple she can see what goes on in the street. She sees particularly, with increasing horror and a dawn of love, the slow death that is being dealt out to her Libyan—naked and bleeding, stripped of his armour—by the populace along the triumphal way. Just before he dies their eyes meet. She rises from her wedding feast, drains her glass, and falls dead.

This is where the novel ends. Flaubert's tone here is self-congratulatory. He is pleased with the operatic story he has added to Polybius, and pleased especially with the way he has made it end. But his story, shallow, never convincing, always a fabrication, seemingly derivative, undermines the greater labour of the book: the historical superstructure, the too-careful attempt to reconstruct the topography and architecture and religion of Carthage. It is a dreadful misjudgement.

To compare *Salammbô* with the second chapter of *Madame Bovary,* to look at the narrative style and the texture of the language, is to wonder about the misjudgement. The details cannot be compared: one set of details—living, easy—comes from the writer's mind and memory; the other set comes from books or—their equivalent—from travel undertaken (after he had begun to write his book) to look at landscape and get atmosphere. The books are dissimilar; the techniques are dissimilar.

Salammbô, the fruit of much research, is the more considered. The second chapter of *Madame Bovary* is more instinctive, so instinctive that one can wonder whether the writer planned all his effects. But of course he did; and it is possible, though it is hard, to see this writer in the second book. If you read the difficult descriptive passages slowly, and more than once, if you read them until you get to know them almost as well as the writer knew them (in isolation from the rest of the book, which slightly falls away), you begin to feel something of the writer's labour and something of his care. But this time you can also, disquietingly, feel something of his triumph.

Ambition makes a writer reach beyond what he has already achieved. And this is when, out of his security, he can make misjudgements. This misjudgement might have to do with something small, such as a matter of style, a way of writing that has crept up on a writer. Sometimes it is more serious, the very conception of a book. The more the writer feels ill at ease, the harder he tries, using all the resources of his talent, to prove his point; and then, seeing him suffer to do so, one is more than half in sympathy with him.

THE CLASSICAL HALF VIEW

THE MISTAKE IN *Salammbô* is in taking an ancient text like Polybius's, which is good and brisk on its own terms, and thinking that if the gaps can be filled in it will make a whole. Polybius is a man of the ancient world and he is writing for people like himself who possess the whole apparatus of ancient civilisation: the art of war and the tools of war, ideas of human association, of obedience, slavery and punishment, the pleasures of the arena. To "fill in" Polybius, to spell out all the things he leaves unsaid, would be to destroy his narrative art and to distort his moral ideas, to lose his essence. To do a modern account of the mercenary war would call for another kind of narrative. In that narrative Polybius might be an important witness, but we will need another kind of morality, where our contemporary ways of feeling are acknowledged.

Caesar is famous for his brevity. But he leaves so much out in his year-by-year report on the conquest of Gaul we are not always sure what he is saying. He was writing for people like himself who would have known about ancient warfare (so much of it hand to hand) and wouldn't want everything spelled out (unlike modern schoolboys who in their first year of Latin have to learn the compressed vocabulary of war without fully understanding what the words can open out to mean).

In the beginning Caesar is formal. He takes his time, writing with something like fascination about the religion, manners, and social organisation of the Gallic tribes; he is like a man settling down to writing history for literary glory. But then the war develops; he becomes rougher; and we begin to learn more. In the second year, when the fortress town of the Atuatici is stormed, he decides to sell all the inhabitants by auction. One man or one group buys the lot, and Caesar hears later that the number of people sold was fifty-three thousand. That one man or group bought so many is to Caesar an oddity, and he reports it as such in his dry way, in one sentence.

We don't know where the Atuatici auction took place. Was it in the conquered town? Were the prospective buyers summoned to Caesar's camp? (They couldn't have been very far away.) Was there, after the others had dropped out, some deal with the powerful buyer, man or syndicate (clearly known to Caesar), who had then within a limited time (as in modern auctions) to take away the goods, rendering an account to

Caesar? We don't know. Caesar tells us no more about the commercial arrangements of his campaigning. But they would have been complicated. Caesar made a fortune out of Gaul; and his commercial arrangements would alter the picture we have of Caesar on the march.

The merchants, so quickly and powerfully present among the defeated Atuatici, would have been *equites*, Roman knights, not aristocrats, not senators, but money people, almost a caste, making a killing here as in other places out of the spread of Roman power. They would have had facilities for taking control of those many thousands of prisoners, taking them from camping place to camping place in hostile territory, guarding them, feeding and watering them, and then walking them back to Rome or wherever they were to be sold off. They would have been like a separate army. It would have been nice to have a glimpse of this side of things from Caesar; it would have completed the picture; our modern sensibility requires it. But we are told nothing. We have only Caesar's bare line about the numbers.

In later chapters, about other campaigns, the picture fills out. We hear of traders camping at the foot of the Roman rampart during a hard engagement; we also hear of an *eques*, a knight, who has been appointed head of the commissariat by Caesar; and then we are told about *equites* settled in Gallic towns. They would have known when they were needed in Caesar's camp.

Roman readers, many of whom would at one time have been in the army, would have had no trouble with Caesar's austere narrative; they would have found it complete as it is.

They would have known how to read the shorthand. In 53 BC, after he had put down yet another dangerous rebellion, Caesar ordered that Acco, the "instigator" of the trouble, should be executed "in the ancient Roman manner." He says no more; and if you don't know what he means his polite way with words leaves you imagining horrors.

In the eighth and last chapter of *The Gallic War* the ancient Roman manner of execution is made clear. Interestingly, this chapter was not written by Caesar (events at Rome had grown too tense), but by his colleague Hirtius; and it is left to Hirtius to describe plainly the execution Caesar had decreed for Gutuater, yet another "warmonger" and instigator of rebellion. The man was already out of his mind with fear; he was in hiding and no one among his tribe knew where he was. Caesar asked for him to be found and delivered up. The man was found. When he was brought to Caesar the soldiers pressed around. They thought Gutuater was responsible for their recent sufferings and losses and though they knew that Caesar didn't like harsh punishments, they wanted Gutuater executed, clearly in the ancient Roman way. "Accordingly," Hirtius writes, in one sentence, "he was flogged to death and his head cut off." That was the ancient Roman way. It was all in the day's work for the legionaries.

Ancient warfare was dreadful. "They killed," Caesar writes of his men at the end of a successful engagement in Gaul, "until their right arms were tired"—and the precision about the right arms gives a picture and tells the full, awful story. Perhaps because of the general dreadfulness the Latin vocabulary of war, created by an especially militarist people, seems strangely abstract. Words are counters, perhaps, for military men too; and, in their compression, their containing much more than we know or wish to say, the words of war seem separate from their meanings.

Even an idea like "foraging"—which the schoolboy encounters pretty soon—has to be taken on trust; we don't quite know what is meant. The Roman readers of *The Gallic War* would have known more. They would have known what was being foraged for, and they would have known about the rituals or regulations for storage. They would have known that the legions travelled with their servants, and that it was often these servants (in at least one case mistaken by the enemy for legionaries) who were sent out of the camp to forage and were no great loss when they were killed or, as once in Gaul, captured, tortured, chained, and starved.

Roman readers would have had a clear picture in their head of the procedures in camp when on Caesar's orders the six thousand men of the Verbigeni clan, associated with the Helvetii, were hunted down by the tribes through whose territory they were fleeing to the Rhine, brought back to Caesar, and killed. Six thousand men killed at the same time in a small space, and not in the heat of battle: there would have been cries and groans for a long time, and the ground would have steamed with blood. But there is no blood in Caesar's abstract half-line statement: "they were put to death"—one of the Latin constructions the schoolboy learns early. The Roman reader would have supplied the blood for himself.

There are signs that Caesar grew more brutal in his methods and in his writing as matters in Rome grew more complicated for him, as alliances there became less reliable, and as Gaul showed itself rebellious when it should have been pacified, as he had been writing to the senate. The money side of the war becomes clearer. More prisoners are taken (and would have been disposed of); and the soldiers begin to get their share, one prisoner to each man after the siege of Alesia. After the siege of Avaricum, though, the legionaries are so incensed at what they have endured they prefer to kill the prisoners. This means a loss of money for everybody, but Caesar is admiring. "None of our soldiers," he writes, "thought about making money by taking prisoners." And at the end of the day out of the population of forty thousand people only about eight hundred manage to run away. More work there for the short swords and the strong right arms of the legionaries.

IN 55 BC, when Caesar was dealing with an incursion of Germans across the Rhine; when (to impress the local people) he built and dismantled a bridge over the river; and when he also went on a reconnoitring expedition to Britain; in that busy year for Caesar, Pompey, Caesar's ally and rival, inaugurated his theatre in Rome. It was the first stone theatre in the city. These great Roman generals made money: Pompey had done in the Roman east what Caesar was doing in Gaul.

Building the theatre was not the end of Pompey's expenses. He wished to inaugurate his theatre with five days of animal-hunt shows, two shows a day. That would have cost a great deal of money: assembling the wild animals and their keepers from all parts of the Roman world, transporting them to

Rome, feeding them and keeping them fit until the day of the show, when they were taken up to the arena, to face the long spears of the men who, though one or two might be mangled, were going to kill them. The animals, penned up for many weeks, would have known in the arena, when they saw themselves hedged by the long spears, that they were going to die. Enraged then, they would have thrown themselves on the spear. This was the moment the Roman crowd went to see.

Cicero, the orator-statesman and philosopher, went to all five days of the "games." He wrote to a literary friend in Pompeii about them. The friend was an invalid and was sorry to have missed the great occasion. Cicero wrote to comfort him; and though he thought it wasn't the right thing for him to do, Cicero couldn't help expressing admiration for the big show over which his ally Pompey had taken such trouble and spent so much of his new fortune. Rome in fact had never seen anything like Pompey's games; twice in his letter Cicero said that the games were magnificent. But he knew that a little more was expected of him, and as "a man of culture" he affected a world-weariness about these shows of blood, in which both men and animals died. What pleasure was it, he said, to see a puny human being mangled by a powerful wild animal? And what pleasure to see a splendid animal impaled on a big hunting spear? It might be something to see, as people said; but his friend in Pompeii had seen it all before anyway, and for Cicero himself there was nothing new.

But he went to all the five days, and perhaps (in spite of a law case) twice a day. The last day was the day of the elephants. It was the big day; and now Cicero writes strangely.

The "mob and crowd" were very impressed but didn't express pleasure. The feeling in the theatre was, rather, that the mighty elephant had an affinity with men.

What was Cicero trying to say, or trying not to say? A note in the Loeb translation refers us to Pliny the Elder, who said in his *Natural History* that there were twenty elephants in Pompey's games, and their cries, as they were being speared to death, troubled the Roman audience, who rose and cursed Pompey. Pliny died in the big eruption of Vesuvius in AD 79; so he could not have been an eyewitness of Pompey's games in 55 BC. He was perhaps only recording what might have become a folk memory of the games when, unusually, the Roman arena crowd objected to blood. Cicero could have spoken more plainly. He could have told us more. But he was a friend of Pompey's; he would not have wanted to diminish the event; and so, like Caesar in Gaul, he preferred to use words to hide from what he saw. He preferred to have the half view. It enabled him, in the brutalities of the ancient world, to see and not see.

Five years before this, Cicero had become agitated about a runaway slave belonging to the famous actor Aesopus. Aesopus was a friend, and Cicero wrote about the runaway to his brother Quintus, propraetor in Roman Asia. Licinius, the slave, in the company of Patro, an Epicurean, had posed as a freedman in Athens and then had gone to Asia. He seems to have been making his way as a free man, but then he became over-confident. He went back to Athens and fell into the company of Plato, another Epicurean, who a little later had a letter from Aesopus about his runaway slave. Plato put two and two together, and had poor Licinius arrested. Cicero didn't know whether the runaway had been taken to a jail or a private mill. He wanted his brother to find out, and to send the man back to Rome. Aesopus was "grieved at his slave's criminal audacity" and wanted the man back. "Don't stop to consider what the fellow is worth," Cicero wrote. "He is of no great value. He is a mere nobody."

Slaves at a mill ground corn; it was an immemorial punishment. The mill would have been an everyday sight in the ancient world. There is a mill in the *Odyssey;* there is a mill in the second-century *Metamorphoses* by Apuleius; there is a mill in *Salammbô*. They are all dreadful places. In Flaubert's mill (on Hamilcar's estate) the slaves are muzzled so that they won't eat the flour they are grinding; this is pure Flaubert, cruelty for cruelty's sake. The truest description, which appears to be taken from life, is in Apuleius. The animals are in an awful way, with the hooves of the donkeys overgrown, to add to their torment; and the slaves are disfigured runts, their eyelids half caked with the smoke from the baking ovens, with letters branded on their foreheads and their half-shaved heads, irons on their legs, and their bodies seamed all over with the marks of old floggings. They are covered with dirty flour, the way the athletes in the arena were covered with dust (a detail that brings the arena to life).

It is extraordinary that Cicero could contemplate a man, fairly educated, with social gifts, and recently acting like a free man, committed to that kind of hopelessness. But for Cicero, with his lawyer's instinctive fierceness about slaves and his politician's wish, in a disturbed republic, to maintain social order, Licinius the slave had simply been criminal and audacious to run away, and had put himself beyond the pale.

He deals with this matter in a paragraph. Then he goes on, with Roman political news of 60 BC: "And now let me tell you what you most desire to know. The constitution is completely lost to us . . ."

IF WE HAVE TO define modern sensibility in literature, we can, I suppose, say that it is one that in its assessment of the world brings all the senses into play and does so within a frame of reason. Virgil's big poem, the *Aeneid*, is restricted in many ways, but in its restrictions, its simple landscapes and simpler theology, its celebration of earth rites, its simple ideas of history, it seems to take us straight into the official Roman world view. But it may be that in this poem Virgil was holding himself back; it may be that there was available to him another, more intimate way of looking and feeling—a strangely modern way—that could not be used in formal, imperial work.

At the end of the two-volume Loeb edition of Virgil the editor prints eight minor poems which may or may not be by Virgil. One of these poems is "Moretum." It is a hundred and twenty-four lines, five Loeb pages, and is a work of great beauty. The editor describes it as an idyll, which means a rustic or pastoral scene, though it is like no idyll I know. According to the editor, it is derived from a Greek poem, and is also a reworking of a century-old Latin piece; it has sixty-nine non-

Virgilian words, and is too realistic to be by Virgil. But in the *Georgics,* Virgil's poem about agriculture and country life, there are realistic passages which seem to be drawn from long observation; and Virgil would have known that realism of this kind would not have worked in the formal narrative and artificial landscapes of the *Aeneid.* The point about the authorship of "Moretum" is not really important, however; what is being suggested here is that Virgil would have known about the style of "Moretum," and it would have been a style that was open to him.

The poem is without any supernatural machinery. This immediately makes it closer to the reader. It begins at cock-crow on a winter's dawn. Simylus, who works a smallholding, hears the cock and, lying on his poor bedding on the floor, awakes in the dark and straight away begins to worry about hunger later in the morning.

He stretches out his hand to the fireplace. An ember from last night's fire burns him. He gets up then, takes his lamp, uses a needle to pull out the wick, and holds the lamp at a slant against the coals which still have life; he puffs and puffs to get the wick to catch. It does, but it is not easy. He uses his hand to shelter the flame against draughts, and unlocks the closet door with a key. There is a small heap of corn on the ground. He uses a measure to take what he needs; sets his now faithful lamp (as he thinks of it) on a tiny shelf, which he has put up against the wall for just such a purpose. He is dressed in goatskin. He begins to work his little stone mill, pouring the corn from the top with his left hand, driving the wheel with his right, while the bruised grain runs down the lower stone.

Round and round the wheel goes. He begins to sing a country song, and then from time to time he shouts for Scybale.

She is his only help, and is perhaps a slave, though that isn't said. She is a black African—the only black African I know in Latin literature—and, perhaps because she is unusual, she (unlike Simylus) is described in detail: curly hair, swollen lips, dark (*fusca colore*), broad-chested, her breasts hanging low, her belly flat, her legs thin, her feet broad and flat. Her shoes are torn in many places.

Simylus tells her to put more logs on the fire and heat some cold water. (So far everything in the morning ritual has been physically explained: the dying fire from the night before, the little shelf for the lamp, the storage place in the closet for the grain, the little stone mill. But now some things are left out: we don't know where the water came from and where it was kept, and we don't know where Scybale slept.)

Simylus finishes his grinding, puts the crushed grain in a sieve, and shakes it. The husks remain in the sieve, the pure meal drifts down. This meal he spreads on a smooth table, pours Scybale's hot water on it, packs and kneads the moistened meal until it is hard, from time to time sprinkling salt on it. Now with his palm he flattens the mixture, makes it round, and marks where it is to be divided into four equal portions. Scybale has in the meantime cleared a space in the hearth, and there the morning's flat bread is placed, and covered with tiles and fire, Vulcan and Vesta, so to speak.

(I have no Greek; it was not taught at my school. If Robin Lane Fox hadn't written to me about it, I wouldn't have known that *scybale* was Greek for dung or rubbish. So the poor African woman slave was named for what she was thought to work in; she became "Miss Manure": horrible, this insult lodged in a beautiful idyll.)

Simylus has little in his house to go with his bread. From the ceiling near his hearth no larder hangs with dried and salted bacon. There are only old round cheeses in baskets of woven fennel. But he has a little herb garden outside, watered when necessary by rills near by, and sheltered by willows and reeds. He works in this garden when it rains and on holidays. He has the gardener's skills. He grows cabbage, beet, sorrel, mallows and leeks, lettuce that rounds off a rich banquet, and radishes and gourds. This is not for himself. Every nine days he gets together a load of faggots, which he takes to the town to sell. He comes back light in neck and shoulder and heavy in pocket; he doesn't spend his money on city goods. To curb his own hunger he eats red onions and chives, sharp-tasting nasturtium that pinches the face, and endives. And there is colewort that brings back amorous capacity.

Outside now in his garden Simylus digs his fingers in the earth and pulls out four bulbs or cloves of garlic, adds to this some parsley, rue and coriander. Then in the cottage he sits by the pleasant fire and loudly calls to the maid for a mortar. He peels off the outer skin of the garlic bulbs, lets that skin fall on the floor, puts the garlic and its leaves in the mortar, sprinkles salt on it, adds some salt-hardened cheese, puts on top the parsley, rue and coriander. With the pestle he crushes first the fragrant garlic, then grinds the whole mixture together. The various elements gradually lose their particular strength, the colours blend into one, not green, not white; and then he adds a few drops of oil and a little strong vinegar, stirs the dish, until at last he runs two fingers around the mortar and presses everything together into a ball. This is the "moretum" which, with his flat bread (Scybale has taken it out of the hearth), he will take to the field as his food for the day.

Carefree, now that he has lost his fear of hunger for the day, he puts on his leggings and cap, forces his obedient bullocks under the leather-bound yoke, and drives them to the fields, where they bury the plough in the earth.

THE PHYSICAL DETAILS in this poem, taking nothing for granted, making us see and touch and feel at every point, celebrate the physical world in an almost religious way—lighting the lamp (the Roman wick-and-oil lamp, which never developed through all the Roman centuries), grinding the corn, kneading the dough—and these details turn the smallholder's morning into ritual. This kind of writing will appear two thousand years later in the stories Tolstoy did after learning Greek in mid-life in order to read the epics. But the Roman taste was for the rhetorical, in which what was ordinary could be inflated.

The high style of poetry reached its peak with Virgil and the other poets in the first century BC. What is amazing is how little it developed afterwards. Latin poetry (properly speaking) ended long before the empire ended. The poets of the fourth century play games; they have little to tell us; it is as though the early poets had used up all the high matter of Rome, and there was nothing of that sort left for latecomers.

Of course there was much to observe. We would love to know about life in the late empire; we would love to be taken into the hut of people like Simylus and Scybale; but the poets don't help us now, and all of that is closed to us.

It might seem that satire is outside rhetoric, but, as with the other kind of poetry, the matter of satire was more or less fixed by the early satirists: it could be erotic, or it could deal with the life of the city, or it could rail against the degeneracy that came with Roman wealth. This, absurdly, was the very note struck three hundred years later, near the end of empire, by the soldier and historian Ammianus Marcellinus, when he wrote about the life of the city of Rome. Ammianus had witnessed the Roman defeat at Adrianople, which finally let in the barbarians. But when he came to write about the city of Rome it was as though in spite of the upheavals, the endless bloodlettings, the disappearance of the great families, the tyrannies, the Illyrian emperors, the general remaking of Rome, nothing had changed: so strong was the idea of old literary form, and so pleased was Ammianus at being able to do the approved thing.

The art historian Bernard Berenson was said to be working in his last years on the "deformation of form," the decay of the classical ideal (or the talent to render it in painting or sculpture) in the Dark Ages, and its replacement by Byzantine angularity or worse. Nothing came out of Berenson's interest. It was said that the subject was too big. But it may be that the survey of bad art and the picking out of debased motifs was too repetitive. A rise to achievement makes a better narrative than random decay. Perhaps it was enough for Berenson to raise the subject, which could so easily have been ignored, taken for granted.

The loss of literature in the same period is of comparable interest, and is easier to study in the texts that survive. In the second century Latin prose writing would have seemed alive and developing, able to deal with ever new subjects; yet it very soon was to exhaust itself. Four hundred and twenty years after Caesar there is a reference in Ammianus to an execution in the "old Roman way"; as with Caesar, now deified, there is no explanation. So little has the world moved on. There is still, as in the beginning, the need to use words to hide from reality. In four hundred years language hasn't illuminated a great deal that is new. In the brutality and now the hideous uncertainty of the Roman world—"madness" is the word Ammianus often uses, not only of wild animals in the arena, but also of men, tormenting and tormented—in this world without balance people need more than ever the classical half view, the ability to see and not see.

Shaun
Michael
Samano

August, 2009

Toronto, ON
Canada.

FIVE

India Again: The Mahatma and After

WE GO BACK to India, to the town of Kanpur, to the Indian National Congress conference of 1925. The conference tent was very big. It was more than a hundred yards long and sixty yards wide, and there were seven or eight thousand people sitting on matting on the ground. At the far end was the raised rostrum for speakers and distinguished visitors; they too were sitting on matting.

The fifty-six-year-old mahatma was there, in his strange garb: the tightly tied dhoti, like a diaper, around his waist and upper legs, with a shawl (a concession to the Kanpur winter) over his shoulders. The writer Aldous Huxley, only thirty-one, also on the rostrum (at one session "all but dead of fatigue" after sitting on the floor for six hours), was a witness of the occasion. He mentions the dhoti and the shawl, but he doesn't comment on them; he seems to take them on trust as the scant clothing to be expected of an Indian saint. He doesn't know (he seems to have begun reading Gandhi's autobiography only later) that that excessive simplicity of dress was Gandhi's own idea and would at first have been strange, perhaps outlandish, to many Indians, who looked for greater formality in their politicians.

It was in South Africa, before he became a mahatma, that he began adjusting his costume. In the beginning in South Africa, in the 1890s, in his dealings with the Indian merchants who had called him to South Africa, and with European officials, he had been particular about his dignity as a lawyer (that would have been his London training). Now he thought he should look less like a lawyer and more like the Indian labourers for whom he had become the spokesman. The costume he worked out for himself was a shirt (perhaps a long one), the dhoti, a cotton cloak, and a scarf (which could also serve as a fast-drying towel). It was all of cheap Indian mill cotton, but when he came to India and began to travel third class on the crowded Indian railways he grew to think his many-pieced costume was too fussy and troublesome, and he gave up the scarf and the cloak. The man who appeared raw, so to speak, before Huxley had a history Huxley would not have suspected. Huxley saw him as complete, a Peter the Hermit figure.

In fact, there was no completeness to him. He was full of bits and pieces he had picked up here and there: his mother's love of fasting and austerities, the English common law, Ruskin's idea of labour, Tolstoy's Russian religious dream (Tolstoy who had fathered twenty-five children, twelve of them by serf women), the South African jail code, the Manchester No Breakfast Association. His strong political cause—in South Africa and India—gave an apparent unity to all these impulses, but there was no real unity; the pieces did not fit together; no piece was indispensable. The simple life did not serve the cause of Indians in South Africa. Nor did the school at Tolstoy Farm, where Gandhi played Mr. Squeers and everyone had to do gardening and where, as it turned out, the children had to do most of the hard work, felling timber and digging and carrying. The children didn't like it. "Of course some of them, and sometimes all of them, malingered and shirked." And when Gandhi left South Africa and went back to India, what happened to the farm and the school? Many of Gandhi's smaller and now forgotten experiments, involving the labour of others, were like this, not thought out, unachieved and abandoned, serving no cause, good for the famous man and not for the people who for various reasons had come (or sent their children) to lend a hand.

(And this idea occurs. If, as was more than likely, Gandhi had failed to graft himself on to the Indian political scene when he went back to India in 1915, what would have happened to his famous costume? Would he have stuck to it as a man unknown and would he, out of simple stubbornness, have kept on doing his latrine-cleaning? For how long?)

His intellectual confusion wasn't obvious to Aldous Huxley, but it was there. Take away his political cause and you see it, all the unrelated impulses. It is not easy to enter the culturally denuded mind of the Gandhi who went to England in 1888. He had the most basic idea, a village idea, of Indian religion and the epics, but he didn't know the history of India, not even a school version; he didn't know geography, hardly had a map of the world in his head. He didn't know about books and modern plays, hardly had an idea of news and newspapers. Busy, modern London would have been a horrible shock. He didn't know how to keep his footing; he must have felt he was drowning. The few dancing lessons he took, his violin lessons, and the horrible prospect of his elocution course must have depressed him more than he says. He would have seen how culturally far away he was, and with something like desperation he would then have lost himself in the abstractions of his law studies, cramming, reading right through the English common law and studying Roman law in Latin.

South Africa a few years later showed him that this new world, barely understood, was exceedingly hostile, and even full of physical threat. The shock, the wound, would have been many times greater than the shock of London. He had the law now; it was better than nothing. But he needed more, and so he held on to all the pieces of comfort he could get from European well-wishers and people who came within his orbit, and soon he was a man of many small causes.

These causes, disguising his wound and his primary, Indian cause, attracted many different people, who saw in him their own personal cause. (Though Tolstoy, Russian nationalist though he was, thought that Gandhi's Indian nationalism "spoiled everything.") So Gandhi's many causes made him appear more universal than he was. He came at the right time; the world was oddly vacant; there was room for him; and in 1909 he could get away with the nonsense and anti-modern simplicities of his first book, *Hind Swaraj* ("Indian Home Rule"). The book would not be read in India, not even by scholars (and still hasn't been), but its name would often be taken as a milestone in the independence struggle, and it would be cherished as a holy object. Twenty-five years later, after the Russian revolution, after Hitler, with a world waiting for war, he might have had a harder ride.

And when, forty years or so later, the main cause had been won, and India had become independent, it was those "outside" causes that made it hard for people to know what Gandhi-anism was. Was it the dhoti, the spinning wheel, the homespun, the Thoreau, the Ruskin (what was there for Indians in *Walden* or *Fors Clavigera*?), the sexual abstinence, the vegetarianism, the Christian hymns, the refusal to drink cow's milk, the latrine-cleaning? It was impossible for anyone to be a complete Gandhian; no one could make that pioneer journey again; people had to take the one or two things they liked from the menu. In the main they took the homespun; that was the easiest and most stylish item.

Not many years ago an Indian woman parliamentarian, concerned about Indian cruelty to animals (as Gandhi had been, though only in passing), said that people should stop drinking cow's milk; the animals were dreadfully tormented to produce milk. The newspapers ridiculed the parliamentarian; there were cartoons. But what she was saying was only what Gandhi had said seventy years before. Gandhi drank goat's milk; this was generally known; what wasn't known, or had been forgotten almost as soon as it had been said, was why he didn't drink cow's milk. Gandhi also spoke about the peasant's cruelty towards his bullocks. But this again is something no one in India remembers.

The saintly half-clad figure Aldous Huxley saw on the rostrum in Kanpur in 1925 was not wholly Indian, as Huxley thought. The best part of Gandhi in 1925 had really been made in London and South Africa. And just twenty-five years later he would be out of date, the various pieces of his thought irrecoverable.

THERE WAS A FOOLISH MAN, Vinoba Bhave, who in the early 1950s tried to do a Gandhi repeat. He had been brought up in Gandhi's various ashrams. The mental idleness of those places had softened his brain and entered what might be called his soul. He worked in the kitchen and did the latrines and then sat for so long at his spinning wheel that Gandhi noticed and worried about it. He thought that Vinoba, who was still a young man, should go away and study somewhere. If he didn't he was going to fall ill at the ashram spinning wheel. Vinoba went to the holy city of Banaras, and there he was thought by the devout to have developed fantastic yogic powers.

He had lived for so long as a parasite, and away from the world, that he had become a kind of half-man, and he thought that Gandhi had been like that too. Vinoba had no means of knowing that Gandhi was a man of appetite, and his sexual abstinence hadn't come easily. One idle day in the ashram, some time after Gandhi's death, Vinoba had the idea (or it had been put to him: he had his admirers) that he should take over from the great man. There were the clothes—he could do that. There was the spinning wheel—he could more than do that; he had practised under the master's eye; and it would help pass the time. There was the ashram routine, with even a little (but not too much) latrine-cleaning—that was in his blood. Up to there it was easy.

But even Vinoba could see that he was only an ashram fellow, hidden away, and that Gandhi had been a public man, a national figure, a master of simple but big political gestures (like the spinning wheel itself) that could light up the country. Now, casting about for some big public gesture he might make, Vinoba remembered that Gandhi had done some big walks. In 1946, at the age of seventy-seven, he had done a walk in Bengal during the communal riots just before independence. That hadn't been a successful walk; in fact, it was full of bitterness. But fifteen years before there had been a stupendous and historical two-hundred-mile walk from the ashram in Ahmedabad to the sea. The independence movement had been becalmed for some time, and Gandhi in his Ahmedabad ashram (but not idle) had thought hard and long about what he might do to revivify it. He had arrived at this idea: doing a march to the sea in stages, with the world press looking on, and at the end symbolically making salt, in practice only defying the salt laws (salt was a government monopoly), but at the same time making a big political point and exciting the country afresh.

The full symbolism of the salt march would have eluded Vinoba. He would have known only that the mahatma had walked to the sea and made a little salt. It occurred to him that as the mahatma's successor he should do a little walking himself, or a lot of walking. And, since he couldn't do salt, the cause he chose was land reform. There was actually no need, since the government of independent India had decided to limit the ownership of land to a few acres per person. Vinoba's idea was that he should walk with his crowd in those rural areas where there was distress. India was the land of the mahatma, and Vinoba thought that people with land would be moved by his walk and by the religious frenzy around it to give a little of what they had.

But land couldn't be given just like that; it wasn't like a cup of rice or wheat or flour that could be poured into the mendicant's sack. A gift of land required deeds and surveyors and lawyers. Vinoba hadn't thought of that. He wasn't Gandhi; he had no legal organisation that could deal with that side of his walk; he had only a devout mob with him, gaining merit by being with the holy man. And so it happened that after the ecstasy created by his passage through an area, with the promises of so many acres for the landless, nothing was done when the procession moved on and blood cooled.

The walk and the camps were a riot, according to a simple-minded Italian priest who, looking for illumination in India, went and walked with Vinoba. It wasn't quite the white-clad choric procession he might have expected, classically draped, grave and mute behind the great man, and at a respectful distance from him. There was a noisy rustic mob at Vinoba's heels. The Italian had to dig deep into his reserves of forbearance, and he came up with the idea that there was "the innocence of the fart" in the country people running after Vinoba. The racket in the camp in the evening was hard to endure, with many shouted conversations going on at once and much farting and belching. But *Time* was impressed. It put Vinoba on its cover ("I have come to loot you with love").

So great was the enthusiasm for this successor to Gandhi that someone announced the creation of a university for the movement. Money was collected, and some time later people began to ask questions about the university. What were its courses? Who were its professors? Where was its campus going to be? When these questions were put to Vinoba he sensed that something had gone wrong, that he had been outrun by his fame; and he could only babble. He said, "The ground is there and I have had a well dug in it. The passer-by will be able to draw a bucket of water and drink his fill." When he was pressed in less mystical or poetic words, he would say again what he had said; and his questioners knew that the walker from the ashram was no Gandhi, was completely at sea in the middle of his movement; and they left him alone.

It took some time for the excitement about Vinoba's land-gift scheme to die down. But there was disappointment that India, so soon after independence, hadn't been able to support a second mahatma. People who had not gone into the first mahatma's origins and career saw it as a sign of the moral decay of the country. It is what often passes in India for thought: "I am all right, the country is rotten."

There was, happily, a later career for Vinoba, not as a reformer, not as a wise man, but as a kind of holy fool, someone politicians at the very top wished to be photographed with and whose blessing they wished to have.

And still from time to time in the Indian press there is a cry for the Gandhians of today, and the regret that what had been "the greatest mass movement in history" should have vanished so completely. The unspoken feeling is that Gandhi grew out of the Indian soil and the people who came after have turned away from wisdom that was open to them. There is little understanding that Gandhi had been created by the cultural incompetence of his three years in London and then by his embattled twenty years in South Africa; those extraordinary conditions cannot be repeated. Indians hardly know about the long South African years and are unwilling to read about them. They feel that, being Indians, they possess Gandhi. They don't have to study him; he is inside them and they can find in him what they wish.

THERE IS NO EXPLICIT acknowledgement in Gandhi that in London and South Africa he is dealing with another civilisation. London is simply a big, expensive city where institutions are old and established, and where he has gone to study the law he hopes to practise in India, and where it is hard to get vegetarian food; and South Africa is a place where the laws are bad. Early travellers to Europe from Japan and China and Iran were not like that; they knew that they were looking at another civilisation. Gandhi came from British-ruled India. He knew English, knew about British-style courts and universities, and had seen British architecture in India. He couldn't feel an absolute stranger in London or South Africa. And this feeling of half familiarity made for a deeper confusion, which Gandhi was never able to resolve and finally, sunk in his mahatmahood, stopped worrying about. Nearly all Indians still live in varying degrees with this unacknowledged confusion.

This makes the ambition of Nirad Chaudhuri in *The Auto-*

biography of an Unknown Indian all the more remarkable. His principal subject is the civilisation that, between 1860 and 1910, developed in Bengal with British rule and with the new learning of Europe that British rule brought. Chaudhuri was born in 1897 to an educated middle-class Bengali family who were part of that civilisation. He did nothing noteworthy in his working life. He was not a professional man, and the academic career he dreamed of as an adolescent never materialised. He began this book just before independence came to India in 1947, and it was published in 1951 in England by the grand old house of Macmillan, which had started publishing schoolbooks for India in the 1870s.

The book had a staggering but appropriate dedication: *To the memory of the British Empire in India which conferred subjecthood on us but withheld citizenship; to which yet every one of us threw out the challenge: "Civis Britannicus sum" because all that was good and living within us was made, shaped, and quickened by the same British rule.* This dedication, in small capitals, was spaced out over twelve lines on the page, like a Victorian headstone or commemorative plaque. It ensured attention for the book when it was published. I remember reading Harold Nicolson's admiring review in the *Observer*. And yet, after this balanced beginning, Chaudhuri was claimed by the old Indian cultural confusion resulting from British rule, and ended absurdly; we shall come to that in due course.

His book has, at first, the shape and neutral tone of an ethnographic study. Chaudhuri came from East Bengal (Bangladesh today), and his opening chapters are about the three villages in that watery realm with which he is intimately connected: his father's village, his mother's village, and his ancestral village (where everyone is a relation). The ethnographic tone, which might be modelled on something French, suits Chaudhuri. He is at his best in that mode. It doesn't deny autobiography, but it controls what might become too personal and slack, and it keeps at a distance the polemical and rather hectoring side of his personality, into which after a life of non-doing he is too ready to fall: the wish to display knowledge and settle accounts with the world.

He was very young when he first saw an English person. He and his older brother (who was just learning the English alphabet) had been sent to the bazaar to buy bananas. They were coming back when they saw the Englishman, who might have been Mr. Stapleton, the inspector of schools. The older boy dived into the ditch to hide, to protect his bananas (Englishmen were thought to be particularly fond of this fruit); and his younger brother followed his example. Some years later, when he was nine, he saw his second Englishman, Mr. Nathan, the divisional commissioner, who was coming to the local school to distribute prizes. He was with his wife, and the boys could not get over her blue eyes, her flaxen hair, her skirt, her hat, her high-heeled shoes. Still later, he saw a European baby and was ecstatic over its doll-like quality.

He tells these stories to show that his admiration for English civilisation was separate from his knowledge of English people; and to him there was nothing strange in this separation. The admiration for the civilisation continued as he went through school. Casual details in his narrative speak of a very good British-given education system. To Chaudhuri's remote village or small town, for instance, there once came a benign school inspector who gave a prize-winning small boy (who had shown a drawing of a tiger) money to buy a colour-box; it was the kind of thing only adoring close relations might do.

Chaudhuri in due course went to Calcutta University, where distinguished visiting lecturers (T. R. Glover, Ramsay Muir, Michael Sadleir) came out from England. Chaudhuri went to their lectures. The accent made it hard for him to follow what was said, but he liked to study the faces of these scholars. There is an extraordinary description, written in a tone of worship (such as in the classical world might have been used of the library at Alexandria), of the wonders of the Imperial Library in Calcutta. There were four thousand volumes, only for reference, in the reading room; and a quarter of a million in the library as a whole. Lord Curzon, the viceroy, had built the library up from the much simpler Calcutta Public Library. He had given well-bound folios and quartos from his own collection, and he had brought out an expert from the British Museum to superintend the library's expansion. Calcutta was also where the great Indian Museum was. (When I went there late in 2002 the rooms were closed, or the doors were closed, and the air-conditioning turned off. Calcutta and Bengal have been communist for many years; they do things in their own way, and a consolation for them is that the Madras Museum, far to the south, is a mess, in places a charnel house of dusty sculptured pieces. Communism was what, inevitably, the Bengal renaissance led to in the mid–twentieth century; that was where the new learning ran finally into the sand.)

Chaudhuri became formidably well read. There was never

any complaint from him (as there was later—quite speciously, I feel—from places like the West Indies) about becoming separate from his roots. One of the criticisms of English education in India was that it only created clerks and officials. (There is an echo of this in Aldous Huxley, who says more interestingly, in *Jesting Pilate*, that there is as yet no industry to absorb the many thousands of graduates who leave the universities each year.) Chaudhuri makes another kind of point. He says that people who wished only to become clerks and officials could become just that, passing through the system "quite mechanically"; a few others, "recipients of grace," saw "the original humanistic motive force of the system" and found in their education an introduction to a high civilisation.

Chaudhuri would have said that his English education was part of his education, and this education was part of the new Bengali civilisation in which he felt himself to be rooted. Hinduism had been reformed, given a Christian tinge in its outward aspects; questions of behaviour were ceaselessly discussed. Morality was a living issue; and Bengal, as a result of all these various forces, had the full apparatus of a living literary culture. It had writers and magazines that were important in the life of the middle class. This happened nowhere else in India.

And yet there should have been some feeling in Chaudhuri that he had come from another, more primeval world. Every year in his village (and elsewhere in Bengal and India) there was celebrated the Durga Puja, five days of prayers and rituals ending with a horrible sacrifice of goats and a water buffalo. Chaudhuri describes this sacrifice lyrically, and it is correct for him to do so, since that was how the ritual appeared to him as a child in his village. The poor bleating goat was fixed in a vice; one servant pulled hard on its forelegs, another pulled hard on its hind legs, to make the little animal taut, and then the knife came down on the neck. The head came off and the blood ran, and the priest who had used the knife, wasting no time, put the head with some of the blood in a big plate and offered it at the feet of the goddess Durga.

The killing of the buffalo was messier. The buffalo was bathed and garlanded; three or four servants quickly made it fast; and melted butter was rubbed into the animal's neck to make the skin soft for the scimitar. The scimitar this time was not wielded by the priest but by someone sturdier, since if the scimitar stuck in the animal's neck bad luck would befall the house. As soon as the blow fell everyone in the house, servants, children, relations, visitors, everyone ran to the stricken animal in its death pangs, dabbed their faces and the faces of others with the blood, mixed the blood with the mud of the yard, and for fifteen minutes or so threw bloody mud pellets and balls at one another.

The evening—after this awesome orgiastic event, after what Chaudhuri calls the "alertness" of everybody in the house in the morning—was light-hearted, full of laughter and music. Classical literature is full of animal sacrifice, seldom described in this detail. But this almost certainly was what it would have been like: tense, then orgiastic, then relaxed and fulfilled.

It is astonishing that Chaudhuri could, without strain, have contained so many worlds within himself. But then strain came, with the politics of the nationalist movement, with the new eyes that that movement gave, and everything that was so nicely balanced came tumbling down. There is no politics in Chaudhuri's account of his golden childhood in settled, golden Bengal. Then, quite late in his book, Chaudhuri says that the British had their own areas in Calcutta; the streets there were more elegantly paved than in the Indian areas; there were sections of Eden Gardens where Indians couldn't walk. When Indians (including Chaudhuri) wanted to go aboard the visiting German warship *Leipzig*—this was before the First World War—they were beaten back by policemen with sticks and whips.

This is more than information. This marks a change of mood; the earth here is about to move. "We believed in the second advent of our country and nation with a firmness of conviction which nothing could shake." Forty years later, at the time of the writing of the *Autobiography*, he has another kind of comment to make. "This amazing faith, running counter to all the known facts of history which go to prove that a nation overtaken by decline after once creating a great civilisation never rises again, was to us justified by itself . . ." This is where, going against his earlier, natural emotion of pain and shame, his learning has taken him. This is how he will sit out the great nationalist movement that is about to unfold: offering nothing to anybody, offering no alternative way, knowing only, out of his deep learning, that what is happening around him is historically wrong.

This is where the *Autobiography*, great book though it is, becomes broken-backed; an intellectual flaw becomes a structural flaw. The reader has been led—by what he has read of

Bengal village life, and the journeys along its waterways, and childhood, and Calcutta, and the university—to expect something personal and descriptive (and humorous) about the nationalist movement (with all its great figures), set off perhaps at a lower level by something about Chaudhuri's marriage and his poor jobs. But there is nothing. There is only a long and wordy chapter of historical analysis, which reads like something from another book. As soon as Chaudhuri attempts analysis he becomes vain and mad and begins to use too many words, indifferent to the reader's patience. So it happens that out of a strange, suicidal vanity his once solid book ends in the air, and its better parts have lacked readers.

The error may have begun in Chaudhuri's too golden idea both of his childhood and the new Bengal civilisation which he sees as his own. At the end of the first chapter he states his case, and it is outrageously reactionary. But we are too early in the book to judge it; we read on and forget; and then, when it is almost too late, we are pulled up.

There was violence and sharp practice in the world in which he grew up, he says at the end of the first chapter. But there was also felt to be religion and morality, and justice (like something in the sky, as in the classical world) and order. When things became too bad, justice came down, long-armed and powerful. "It passed by different names among us. The common people still called it the Company, others Queen Victoria, and the educated the Government." With the coming of nationalist agitation, Chaudhuri says, this idea of justice vanished, but the idea of its protective power lived on for some decades. "Today everything is giving way. The thing overhead, once believed to be immutable, has blown up, and the primordial foundation of rock below, on which we thought we had our feet firmly planted, is rotting into dust."

But Chaudhuri's golden past was comparatively new. The Hindu College of Calcutta, which encouraged the Bengal renaissance, was established only in 1817. So the renaissance grew fast. It couldn't stand still when it got to a certain stage. Yet Chaudhuri seems to be saying, in effect, and it is a strange thing to hear from someone claiming historical sensibility, that everything should have stood still in 1910, the last year of virtue—1860 to 1910 is for him the great period of the Bengal renaissance—and that the Company or Queen Victoria should have continued to rule. This is nonsense. But Chaudhuri feels he can say it because, unlike the rest of us, he is a scholar.

He developed this vanity, about being a scholar, when he was quite young. A relation had bought the eleventh edition of the *Encyclopædia Britannica* and had left the set for a few months in the Chaudhuri family home. Chaudhuri loved the appearance and even the smell of the big volumes. He first read with fascination about dogs, and looked at the gorgeous pictures; then, like a child (which is what he was at the time) with an old-fashioned children's *Book of Knowledge*, he jumped about from subject to subject, from guns to ships.

He discovered in himself an immense, easily satisfied curiosity. This pleasurable idleness, which a multitude of children know, he thought was scholarship. It was how he prepared for the BA examination at Calcutta University, reading up on this and that. Miraculously, it worked: bits of his random reading coincided with the questions, and he came first in his group.

But it didn't work with the more rigorous MA examination. He read and read, but he hadn't looked at the prescribed textbooks. And then, a few weeks before the examination, it was too late to do so. He didn't even try. He stayed in his room and made cardboard boxes or jotted down ideas for an Indian national army. In the examination hall, finally, he found himself all at sea. By the third day—the examination was spread over four days—he thought he should give up. He told his mother. He could have done the examination again the following year, but he didn't have the energy. He told his father. His father, who must have watched his son's scatterbrained, unfocused ways with bewilderment and distress, said, "All right." And Chaudhuri was wounded by what he saw as his father's coolness.

It can be said, strange though it may appear, that Chaudhuri cherished this failure. We can see that its cause was not a lack of intelligence, but waywardness, the perversity of a man who (to put it at its simplest) wished to pass an examination without preparing for it. Many of us will have done similar things on other occasions, will have acted with stubbornness in situations where we know that stubbornness can prove nothing; and Chaudhuri might have won some kind of sympathy from us. He doesn't here because of his hectoring manner.

He exalts his rectifiable MA failure into tragedy, finding in it a sign of his own brilliance and too high ambition. He was the man who wished to possess all knowledge, who wished to move far beyond the university syllabus, and for that reason had failed. Yet he doesn't shed his scholar's vanity; he allows it to spoil his book, with his long and bad historical chapter about Indian nationalism. In later writing he continues to hold his tragedy close, to display it; he turns it almost into achievement.

In his second book he writes, "I shall mention the names of four men whom I consider truly learned. They are Mommsen, Wilamowitz-Moellendorf, Harnack, and Eduard Meyer. When young and immature I cherished the ambition of being the fifth in that series. So I could not have been very modest. But a standard is a standard." Mommsen we know: the historian of Rome, the second winner of the Nobel Prize. But who is Wilamowitz-Moellendorf? (Here Chaudhuri tripped me up. Much later I was to learn, to my shame, that Wilamowitz was not only a very great editor of classical texts, but also—though little known in England, his books not easily available—a figure of authority in the European cultural life of his day.) Chaudhuri's list of learned names is more than impressive. In Calcutta it would have been out of this world, a piece of display in itself, encouraging the reader to feel that Chaudhuri is being unfair to himself and may indeed be the fifth in the series.

To fail the Calcutta MA is not the end of the world for someone wishing to be a scholar. It is an affectation in Chaudhuri to pretend that it is; it might even be an excuse to give up. He could have done the examination again; and if he didn't have the energy to do so just then, there were all the writing years ahead, when he could have redeemed himself. He could have done better work in the two analytical chapters about Indian history that spoil the *Autobiography*. A scholar would have set aside grand theories and been more focused, would have moved more carefully; would not, to state the simplest thing first, have left out the thousand years of Indian Buddhism; would have known that querulous ideas on the Indian hatred of foreigners, this hatred tainting the ten later centuries of Indian history (centuries in the main of Indian defeat), cannot be hung on selective quotations from a tenth-century Arab writer; and on personal prejudice.

Personal prejudice can be amusing in the autobiographical mode; Chaudhuri himself uses it to great effect in his near-ethnographic chapter on life in Calcutta. Prejudice sets him alight. His jaundiced words have a humorous edge then (as they had for me forty years ago, when I first read the *Autobiography*). It was only later that I began to feel that the humour and irony I saw were perhaps not intended, that the writer's prejudice was deadly serious, that he was a man caught in a web and speaking out of pain.

There are perhaps three references in the *Autobiography* to the writer's small size; and he was, indeed, very small, almost dwarfish, some inches shorter than his father, who (he says) was just under five feet six, the Bengali average. Somerset Maugham, a small man, says somewhere that the world looks different to a small man. The world would have looked very different to Chaudhuri.

Chaudhuri, in spite of all the great names he takes, was not a scholar. He had no idea what scholarship meant. He held on to the idea only because it was the main part of his self-esteem. Take that away and he would have been completely lost. The success of esteem of the *Autobiography* (justified success: it is a great book for four hundred out of its five hundred pages) enabled Chaudhuri to keep on writing. Being Chaudhuri, he thought success had come to him not for his picture of East Bengal and Calcutta between 1890 and 1920, but for his hundred pages of "scholarship," his ideas about the history of India; and the later books magnified his flaws.

The thesis of his second big book was that Indians were really ancient "Europeans" (he never fixes these strange people in geography or time) who had been denatured by the pitiless climate. Again, he quotes from his tenth-century Arab (Alberuni, a good man). And, in final support of his absurd case, he claims, in a very Indian way, the privilege of age: "I am old [he was only sixty-eight when this second book was published, and there were quite a few more books to come], and I cannot spend the few years that are left to me tilting at theories which I have taken a lifetime to outgrow."

Still later, there was yet another poor book, this time about the life of the nineteenth-century Sanskritist Max Müller, who had edited the famous *Sacred Books of the East* series. Chaudhuri, now being pampered as a scholar in some quarters, had been given access to some family papers of Müller. But the life of Müller was a very big subject. It had ramifications. It went far beyond the papers Chaudhuri had been given. To be properly done, this study had to take in nineteenth-century Germany, the British Empire in India, the decay of Indian learning, the early orientalists, the Sanskrit idea and the Aryan idea in Europe, the self-regarding academic world of nineteenth-century Oxford.

In a rhetorical passage in the *Autobiography* Chaudhuri had defined his ideal of scholarship, the rhetoric, as so often with

Chaudhuri, suggesting that he had attained the ideal or was within striking distance. "I should . . . have thought that the editing of one text with elegant finality would be a creditable achievement for a decade's hard work. The contribution of a volume or two to a collection like the great *Acta Sanctorum* of the Bollandists, or the *Rolls Series*, or the *Corpus Inscriptionum Latinarum* would . . . have appeared to me as the very summit of ambition and happiness."

It might have been thought that Chaudhuri now had his chance as a scholar, with the Müller book. But Chaudhuri didn't know what to do. He loved the idea of scholarship. Like a kind of Buddhist monk, so to speak, he loved the incantation of the great names of books and their creators. All he could do with the Müller was to go into the family papers and present them flatteringly, in gratitude, almost, for the courtesy done him.

I read no more Chaudhuri after that. But something extraordinary was happening. As Chaudhuri's intellectual worth was declining his reputation in England was rising. It was because of that formal, twelve-line dedication in the *Autobiography* "to the memory of the British Empire in India." The news of the dedication spread slowly; there were always a few more important people who, without feeling the need to read any more of the difficult book, were ready to declare for Chaudhuri. They managed to bring him over to England in extreme old age; he settled in Oxford and celebrated his hundredth birthday there.

He had turned his back on the Indian nationalist movement, on Gandhi and Nehru and all the rest. He couldn't have dreamed of this Oxford apotheosis after the Calcutta MA failure and during the long years afterwards of poverty and unhappiness in India. It would have seemed to him a just reward for his dream of scholarship, for standing by his ideas, for enduring.

I saw a photograph of him in his Oxford days: sitting contentedly in an armchair, an Indian regency figure, dwarfish and shrunken and elderly, in a ruched shirt. At the other pole from the half-naked Gandhi, fifty-six years old, in his made-up Indian costume, whom Aldous Huxley saw at the Indian National Congress in Kanpur in 1925. Two solutions to the same problem: fitting one civilisation to another.

SIXTY YEARS AFTER independence that problem is still there. India has no autonomous intellectual life. Of the many millions whom independence has liberated a fair proportion now look away from India for ultimate fulfilment. They look in the main to Britain and the United States. They look especially to the United States. Immigration rules have changed; but the place is still not crowded out with Indians. That is where the better jobs are, where Indians are well thought of, and that is where people of a certain level wish to live and marry—and make cookies and shovel snow off the pavement in winter—and educate their children.

As much as Chaudhuri did (though he kept it quiet, almost until the end), they wish to shake India off, shake off what they see as the retarded native element in dhotis and caste-marks, temple-goers, to use a kind of shorthand, bad at English, and as an element getting bigger and politically more dangerous by the year. In their new setting the people who have got away wish to dress more stylishly. They wish to wear their own contemporary equivalent of Chaudhuri's regency gear. It is their solution to the problem of India, which is really the problem they have with India.

Out of India's improved English education there has come a crop of novels—a fair number are also by Indian expatriates, mainly from the United States—and there is a new one almost every month. These novels are by and large autobiographical. Every Indian who looks within himself finds the matter for a family story, with great characters, *daddyji* and *mamaji* and *nanee* and *chacha,* against a background of the extended Indian family. Since no writer can have two extended families, these novels appear to be rationed, one per writer. One writer, one book: it may not build a literature, but it is a system that allows new writers and new families to come up all the time.

Is this writing just old-fashioned Indian boasting? Or are these books to be seen as part of a new Indian literary awakening, matching Bengal's of a hundred years ago, helping India now to understand its more complicated self, to develop an autonomous cultural life, to bridge the gap between native and evolved? Or do they belong more to the publishing culture of Britain and the United States? The question has to be asked, because no national literature has ever been created like this, at such a remove, where the books are published by people outside, judged by people outside, and to a large extent bought by people outside.

In the nineteenth century Dostoevsky and Turgenev and

Gogol and Herzen lived for some time outside their native Russia; but they wrote in Russian for Russian readers and (for all of them except Herzen) Russia was where they were published and had their readers. Russia was where their ideas fermented.

Nineteenth-century Russian writing created an idea of the Russian character and the Russian soul. There is no equivalent creation, or the beginning of one, in Indian writing. India remains hidden. Indian writers, to speak generally, seem to know only about their own families and their places of work. It is the Indian way of living and consequently the Indian way of seeing. The rest of the country is taken for granted and seen superficially, as it was even by the young Nehru, until some desperate, ragged villagers, in the middle of an angry agrarian movement that no one in the towns nearby knew about, marched to Allahabad, Nehru's home town, in June 1920 and asked him to come to their villages and see the conditions in which they lived.

The education of the new Indian writers—and nowadays some of them have even been to writing schools—also gets in the way. It seems to them they have the most enormous choice when, in imitation of the successful people who have gone before, they settle down to do their own book. They are not bursting with a wish to say anything; nothing is going to force itself out in its own way; they are guided in the main by imitation. Should they be Irish or German and indulge in wordplay? Should they be South American and see magic everywhere? Should they be like the late Raymond Carver and pretend they know nothing about anything? Or should they simply talk it over with their teacher at the writing school? This is where India begins to get lost. The writing school's India is like the writing school's America or Maoist China or Haiti.

India has no means of judging. India is hard and materialist. What it knows best about Indian writers and books are their advances and their prizes. There is little discussion about the substance of a book or its literary quality or the point of view of the writer. Much keeps on being said in the Indian press about Indian writing as an aspect of the larger modern Indian success, but literary criticism is still hardly known as an art. The most important judgements of an Indian book continue to be imported.

As much as for Gandhi, born in 1869, and for Chaudhuri, born in 1897, India's poverty and colonial past, the riddle of the two civilisations, continue to stand in the way of identity and strength and intellectual growth.

July 2005–October 2006

ALSO BY V. S. NAIPAUL

AMONG THE BELIEVERS

On the basis of his seven-month journey across the Asian continent, V. S. Naipaul explores the life, the culture, and the ongoing ferment inside four nations of Islam: Iran, Pakistan, Malaysia, and Indonesia. In this brilliant account, Naipaul depicts an Islamic world at odds with the contemporary world and fueled by an implacable determination to believe.

Current Affairs/978-0-394-71195-9

AN AREA OF DARKNESS

A classic of modern travel writing, *An Area of Darkness* is V. S. Naipaul's profound reckoning with his ancestral homeland and an extraordinarily perceptive chronicle of his first encounter with India. Traveling from the bureaucratic morass of Bombay to the ethereal beauty of Kashmir and a sacred ice cave in the Himalayas, Naipaul encounters a dizzying cross section of humanity and develops strikingly original and passionate responses to the subcontinent.

Travel/978-0-375-70835-0

A BEND IN THE RIVER

V. S. Naipaul takes us deeply into the life of one man—an Indian who, uprooted by the bloody tides of Third World history, has come to live in an isolated town at the bend of a great river in a newly independent African nation. Naipaul gives us the most convincing and disturbing vision yet of what happens in a place caught between the dangerously alluring modern world and its own tenacious past and traditions.

Fiction/Literature/978-0-679-72202-1

BETWEEN FATHER AND SON

In 1950, V. S. Naipaul, aged seventeen, took a two-week journey by steamer and arrived in Oxford, England, a world utterly removed from the one he had longed to escape and to which he would never really return. This collection of letters between a sacrificing father and his determined son gives us an intimate view of Naipaul's for-

BEYOND BELIEF

Fourteen years after the publication of his landmark travel narrative *Among the Believers*, V. S. Naipaul returned to the four non-Arab Islamic countries he reported on so vividly at the time of Ayatollah Khomeini's triumph in Iran. *Beyond Belief* is the result of his five-month journey through Indonesia, Iran, Pakistan, and Malaysia. In extended conversations with a vast number of people, including a rare survivor of the martyr brigades of the Iran-Iraq war and an intellectual training as a Marxist guerrilla, Naipaul deliberately effaces himself to let the voices of his subjects come through.

Current Affairs/978-0-375-70648-6

THE ENIGMA OF ARRIVAL

The story of a writer's singular journey—from one place to another, from the British colony of Trinidad to the ancient countryside of England and from one state of mind to another—this is perhaps V. S. Naipaul's most autobiographical work. Yet it is also woven through with remarkable invention to make it a rich and complex novel.

Fiction/Literature/978-0-394-75760-5

GUERRILLAS

On a troubled Caribbean island—where Asians, Africans, Americans, and former British colonials coexist in a state of suppressed hysteria—a white man arrives with his mistress, an Englishwoman inflamed by fantasies of native power and sexuality, unaware of the consequences of her actions. Together with a young mulatto leader of the "Revolution," they act out a gripping drama of death, sexual violence, and political and spiritual impotence that illuminates the ravages of history on individual lives.

Fiction/Literature/978-0-679-73174-0

HALF A LIFE

Half a Life is the story of Willie Chandran, whose father turned his back on his brahmin heritage and married a woman of low caste—a disastrous union he would live to regret. As an adult, Willie's flight from the travails of his mixed birth takes him to London, where, in the shabby haunts of immigrants and literary bohemians of the 1950s, he tries to contrive a new identity. His struggle to defeat self-doubt and become a writer bring him to the brink of exhaustion,

A HOUSE FOR MR. BISWAS

All his life, Mr. Mohun Biswas has been trying to achieve some semblance of independence, only to face a lifetime of calamity. Shuttled from one residence to another after the drowning of his father, Mr. Biswas yearns for a place he can call home. But when he marries into the domineering Tulsi family on whom he indignantly becomes dependent, Mr. Biswas embarks on an arduous and endless effort to weaken their hold over him and purchase a house of his own.

Fiction/Literature/978-0-375-70716-2

IN A FREE STATE

It begins as a simple car trip through Africa. Two English people—Bobby, a civil servant with a guilty appetite for African boys, and Linda, a supercilious "compound wife"—are driving back to their enclave after a stay in the capital. But in between lies the landscape of an unnamed country whose squalor and ethnic bloodletting suggest Idi Amin's Uganda. And the farther V. S. Naipaul's protagonists travel into it, the more they find themselves crossing the line that separates privileged outsiders from horrified victims.

Fiction/Literature/978-1-4000-3055-2

ALSO AVAILABLE

The Middle Passage, 978-0-375-70834-3
India, 978-1-4000-3075-0
Literary Occasions, 978-1-4000-3130-6
The Loss of El Dorado, 978-1-4000-3076-7
Magic Seeds, 978-0-375-70727-8
Miguel Street, 978-0-375-71387-3
The Mimic Man, 978-0-375-70717-9
The Mystic Masseur, 978-0-375-70714-8
The Nightwatchman's Occurrence Book, 978-0-375-70833-6
A Turn in the South, 978-0-679-72488-9
Vintage Naipaul, 978-1-4000-3400-0
A Way in the World, 978-0-375-70730-8

VINTAGE INTERNATIONAL